ACKNOWLEDGMENTS

I am dedicating this book to the three closest girls in my life who continue to inspire me and encourage me, my mother Daisy, and my two sweet daughters Madelaine and Annika.

A special thank you to everyone who contributed with knitting the samples and finishing them in such a timely and professional manner: My daughter Madelaine, my mother Daisy, my business partner Debbie Wenclawiak and my dear friends Barbara and Richard Wagner, Cassie Reilly, Christen Parczyk, Lori Giampolo, Margie Rex, Nancy McIlrath, and Pam Maiaroto. Also, I want to thank Kathleen and Nick Greco for their guidance and dedicated work in developing this book.

Finally, thank you to my loyal customers and staff who continue to ask me good questions while directing our new trends in knitting.

–Maria Williams
Stitch Inn

Creative Director *Kathleen Greco Dimensional Illustrators, Inc.*

Executive Editor *Nick Greco Dimensional Illustrators, Inc.*

Design and Typography *Deborah Davis Deborah Davis Design*

Knitwear Designs *Maria Williams Stitch Inn*

Fashion Photographer *Joe VanDeHatert V Studio*

Knitting Techniques and Yarn Photography *Kathleen Greco Dimensional Illustrators, Inc.*

Contents

Maria Williams

746.432

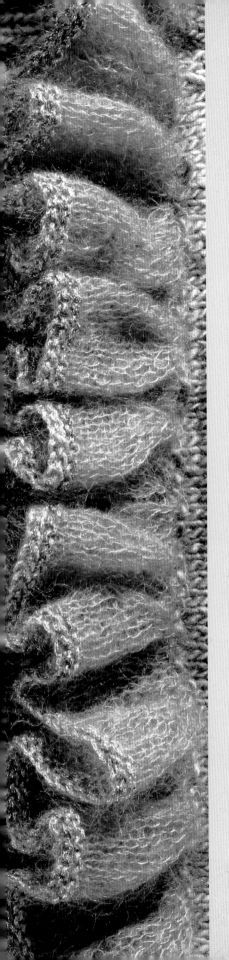

INTRODUCTION

Chic Knits takes the guesswork out of choosing the perfect yarns, and teaches you the secrets of applying conventional knitting techniques in new and innovative ways. Many of the design ideas feature fashion yarn as a decorative border. The fur trim added to our basic Template Poncho creates a unique chic knit. The Domino Shawl and Sampler Jacket are also trimmed with soft furry yarns along the hemlines. In addition to fur, ruffles in contrasting yarns add a romantic flair to an otherwise basic garment. There are two ruffle alternatives featured in the Ruffle Capelet and the Faraoese Shawl. Another focal point is the yoke of the sweater, allowing for some flattering novelty yarns near the face. Use a shimmering yarn as in the Dressy Yoke Top, a ribbon yarn as in the Openwork Pullover, or a soft faux fur found in the Chameleon Sweater.

Knitting with coordinating yarns offers a plethora of design and texture possibilities. Hold multiple strands together as in the Shaped Fur Poncho, Dropped Stitch Poncho and Cuddly Pullover, or alternate yarns in directional rows shown in the Diagonal Poncho, Domino Shawl, and Poncho with Sleeves. You can choose to alternate the novelty yarns while holding one basic yarn throughout in the backdrop—allowing for bigger needles and a firmer fabric. This technique is shown in the Backdrop Pullover and the Long Chenille Vest. Create a one-of-a-kind Ruana Stash Poncho using your leftover yarns by coordinating and hand tying multiple strands together on big needles. Understanding gauge enables you to bridge from one gauge to another while knitting—as shown in the Ruffle Capelet, and the Sampler Jacket.

Reflecting on new, softer styles, I've focused on shoulder shaping to create comfortable fitting garments that stay in place. I have shortened the Faraoese Shawl and accented it with a ribbon ruffle. The little Black Dressy Cape is a must-have wrap, knit with endless yarn possibilities. For a different angle, try the short row technique as shown in the Mink Fur Cape. Try my simple dropped stitch technique to knit an Openwork Poncho that will hold its shape. Wear it as a beach cover-up for a smart new look.

Girls never have too many bags, and we do love knitting our bags. I've featured three felted bags in a variety of sizes and styles. The Felted Chenille Bag has an attractive crushed velvet look. The spacious Messenger Tote and Jazz Bag add more knitting after felting to enhance the design. For evening wear, the blue Vintage Purse features a ribbon pouch in a Victorian silver frame. An urban chic accessory, the Fur Loop Bag is perfect for any party.

Consider these designs as template patterns that offer you a blank canvas to color with your choice of yarns. The key is to collect yarns that appeal to you, and create unique wearable art. Experiment with swatches and you'll discover how much fun it is to play with different yarn combinations.

Chic Knits teaches you the essentials of fine knitting and gives you the confidence to create fun fashion knitwear.

–Maria Williams

Knitting Techniques

The techniques in this chapter were chosen to answer the many questions knitters commonly ask. My aim is to shed light on their use and teach you how to make your knitting experience rewarding and successful. I have included trusted skills such as the Long Tail Cast On, Working with Stitch Markers, the Lasso and Picking Up Stitches, as it is worth investing the time to learn these techniques. I also discuss valuable techniques to raise your knitting skills to the next level; these include Bridging Different Gauges, Twisted Stitches, Slipped Stitches and the 3-Needle Bind Off.

The Cable Cast On technique is recommended for projects that require casting on several stitches at the beginning of a row. For casting on to circular or double pointed needles, review Joining in the Round. Keep an accurate stitch count by learning to Count Rows When Shaping. One of the best techniques for making eyelets or lacework is the Yarn Over. Master the use of a Cable Needle to form beautiful twisted stitches. And for a cool alternative for your knitwear, learn the Felting Wool method and how to Bridge Felt with Knitting.

For finishing, Blocking helps ensure a proper fit, while Crocheting Seams makes seaming easier. See how to make decorative Loops and Self-Made Buttons to accent any project. Finally, the Abbreviations list explains the knitting language used throughout this book. Master these practical techniques and you will become a happier knitter!

CABLE CAST ON

The following patterns use this technique: Poncho with Sleeves, Ruffle Capelet, Faraoese Shawl, and Domino Shawl.

This technique is recommended for projects that require casting on several stitches at the beginning of a row, for example; the Poncho with Sleeves pattern. It is also preferred when casting on a large number of stitches for shawls and ruffles. The finished edge will be both firm and elastic. This cast on technique is not recommended for drop stitch patterns.

Make a slipknot leaving a 6" (15cm) tail, and place on LH needle. Insert RH needle as if to knit, wrap yarn around needle and pull through but do not drop the stitch off LH needle. Bring LH needle forward and insert it into stitch on RH needle from right to left, and slip stitch to the LH needle (picture 1).

2.

Insert RH needle between two stitches on LH needle (picture 2), draw new stitch through and transfer as before to LH needle. Repeat until desired number of stitches has been cast on.

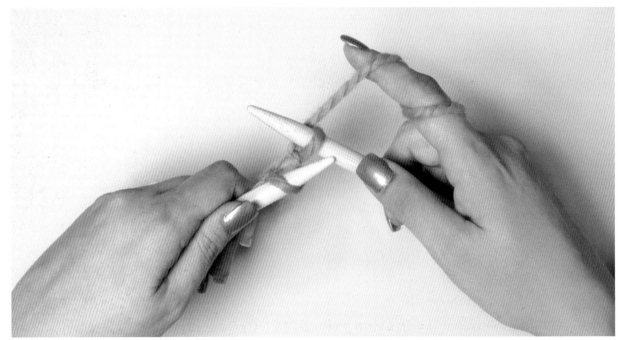

1.

LONG TAIL CAST ON

The following pattern uses this technique:
Dropped Stitch Poncho.

The long tail cast on is always a good technique when starting a new project. It makes a firm yet elastic edge that is perfect for knitwear. This technique is a recognized favorite and has earned many names including Double Cast On and Two Strand Cast On. Start by making a slipknot leaving a long tail. The question I hear often is "How long of a tail do I need?" Be generous, and use the following rule of thumb: Take your 6" (15cm) tail and add 3 times the width of the fabric you're about to make. Depending on your pattern, the width can be found on a schematic or you may have to extract the information from the pattern by working some simple math: Take the number of stitches to cast on divided by the stitch gauge per inch, and you have the width in inches.

Place a slipknot on RH needle and bring left thumb and index fingers between the two tails from back to front. Spread the fingers wrapping the short tail over the thumb and the long tail over the index finger. Close remaining fingers around both tails and hold secure. Stretch the needle up and forward to sit in front of the left hand. You have the correct grip if you see the strand around the thumb forming a cross. Insert the needle under the yarn held by the thumb, then turn the needle to catch the yarn from the index finger as shown.
Note: Reach over the yarn to catch it. Do not pick the yarn as if you're crocheting. Draw the yarn through the loop on the thumb toward you and watch a new stitch appear on your needle. Release the loop off the thumb, pull yarn taut, and repeat by adjusting the grip in your hand.

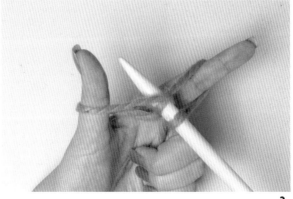

1.

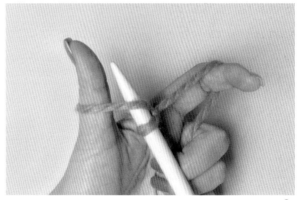

2.

3.

JOINING IN THE ROUND

The following patterns use this technique: Ruffle Capelet, Chameleon Sweater, Dressy Yoke Top and Felted Chenille Bag.

To work in the round, you must cast onto circular or double pointed needles. Choose the proper length circular needle for the number of stitches you wish to cast on. In the case of very small rounds, work with double pointed needles. To join in the round, cast on and place the needle with the yarn attached in your RH. Holding the needle in your RH, run your LH fingers around the cast on edge untwisting the round until it lays flat with the cast on edge facing into the circle, (picture 1).

Place a stitch marker on the RH needle to mark the beginning of the round. Insert the needle into the first stitch on the LH needle and throw the yarn from the RH, (picture 2). You've

2.

carried the yarn across the gap and joined in the round. Pull the yarn taut for the first two stitches of every round. Make sure the stitches are not twisting for several more rounds until you see the fabric is laying flat with the right side facing.

1.

WORKING WITH STITCH MARKERS

The following patterns use this technique: Template Poncho, Shaped Fur Poncho, Ruffle Capelet, Faraoese Shawl, Domino Shawl, Dressy Yoke Top, and Cape, Sampler Jacket, Felted Chenille Bag, Felted Messenger Tote, and Felted Jazz Bag.

Knitters love to knit, and the less time we need to concentrate on knitting the happier we are. Using stitch markers in our work relieves us from counting every step of the way as we're shaping our fabric. The markers serve as road signs to remind us to slow down and pay attention to the pattern. We use them frequently for marking built in seams when increasing or decreasing. When working in the round, we recommend using a different color marker for the beginning of the round to tell you when you've completed the round. They can also be used for identifying

2.

which stitches belong to a specific section of the work, as for the back, front, and sleeves in the Dressy Yoke Top. It is important to choose a marker that is not too large. Be conscious of pulling the yarn taut past the markers or you may leave a trail in the fabric where the markers once stood. Start with a set up row and place the markers (pm) at certain intervals. From this point, we are passing the markers (pm) as we work up to them from the LH needle to the RH needle, (picture 1).

Lock stitch markers are used to remind you which side is the right side of the work. They can also be hooked onto a stitch on the needle to mark it and be moved up to the next row each time you work it (picture 2), as demonstrated in the Domino Shawl pattern.

1.

COUNTING ROWS WHEN SHAPING

The following patterns use this technique: Shaped Fur Poncho, Poncho with Sleeves, Ruffle Capelet, Faraoese Shawl, Chameleon Sweater, Cuddly Pullover, Backdrop Pullover, Dressy Yoke and Cape, Openwork Pullover, and Sampler Jacket.

It is important to interpret knitting instructions correctly before beginning to knit. Let's clarify an often asked question "What does it mean to increase at the beg and end of every 6th row?" You should count each row as you complete it. First, place a marker on the right side of the work (hang a marker in the fabric) to help you keep track. Second, use a row counter, and third, keep a tab on notepaper. Work 5 rows even with no shaping. On the 6th row, increase in the first and last stitch. Begin counting from 1 again to continue shaping. Your pattern should give you a checkpoint of how many stitches are left when the shaping is complete.

Stop and count to make sure you are on track. *Hint: If the shaping is always worked on even numbered rows, you know they will always happen on the same side of the fabric.*

Use your fabric marker as a guide to make sure you are shaping on the proper side. This is especially useful if your stitch pattern looks the same on both sides of the fabric as in the Dressy Cape. Don't fear if you lose your notes and your counter, the answer lies in the fabric where the rows can be counted easily.

Lay the fabric on a table, use a needle to poke and count every loop starting at the cast on edge and moving up toward the needle. Don't include the stitches on the needle, as they haven't been worked yet. Stretch the fabric and re-count to make sure. For each row, you pass one bar in the fabric into the next loop. Practice and feel better knowing you will always be able to check your progress. See picture below.

YARN OVER

The following patterns use this technique: Dressy Yoke Top, and Openwork Pullover.

A yarn over (YO) forms an additional stitch on the RH needle using the yarn. Make a basic YO by passing the yarn to the opposite side of the work between the needles, in front to knit (see picture) and in back to purl. Yarn overs create eyelet holes in the fabric. This increase is

commonly paired with a decrease to keep the stitch count the same at the end of the row. The eyelet can be functional, serving as a buttonhole, or a channel for inserting ribbon or elastic, as in the Dressy Yoke Top. The eyelet is always found in lace patterns, and can take on subtle variations depending on which stitch is worked before and after the yarn over. Four yarn over variations are found in the lace work of the Openwork Pullover, and are described under Abbreviations on (p.25).

TWISTED STITCHES

The following patterns use this technique: Dropped Stitch Poncho, Felted Chenille Bag, and Sampler Jacket.

As a right-handed knitter, we knit and purl each stitch so that the right side of the loop is facing us on the needle. A twisted stitch is turned the other way with the left side of the loop facing. To knit or purl a twisted stitch, we work through the back loop (tbl). Some patterns twist two

1.

stitches (T2) by working them in reverse order as follows: Knit into the second stitch on the needle (picture 1), then knit into the first stitch (picture 2), slip both stitches off the needle together. T2 is used for mock cables in the Felted Chenille Bag, Sampler Jacket, and throughout the Dropped Stitch Poncho.

2.

CABLE NEEDLE

The following patterns use this technique: Felted Chenille Bag, and Sampler Jacket.

To form a cable twist, work 3 or more stitches in reverse order off the LH needle. Temporarily slip part of the cable stitches onto a cable needle (cn), and bypass them as you work the other part of the cable stitches off the LH needle. Next, work the stitches off the cable needle. Between cable twists, put the cable needle down and pick it up again for the next cable twist. I recommend using the U cable needle over the wing cable needle. Make a point to always slip stitches onto the short end

2.

1.

proper side of the fabric. When held in back, the cable slants to the right. When held in front, the cable slants to the left. This information is important as you check the progress of your work.

of the U cable needle (picture 1), and always work them off the long end (picture 2). This will prevent you from turning the needle and causing an error in your knitting. Cables are usually worked in a smooth yarn which shows the pattern beautifully, but also shows "broken cables" when mistakes are made. It is very important to hold the cable needle on the

C6F   C6B

C4F   C4B

3-st left cross   3-st right cross

See p.24 for Abbreviations

BRIDGING DIFFERENT GAUGES

The following patterns use this technique: Ruffle Capelet, Openwork Pullover, and Sampler Jacket.

The stitch gauge can vary as we're changing stitch patterns or yarns throughout the project. When changing from one gauge to another, we must calculate the difference between the current number of stitches and the next set. We are expected to increase or decrease stitches evenly across one row or round to arrive at the new number of stitches. Use this simple mathematical formula to get the job done: Divide the current number of stitches by the number of stitches needed to increase or decrease.

Example 1. Current number of stitches 76 divided by 32 = 2.375. (32 = the number of stitches to increase or decrease.)

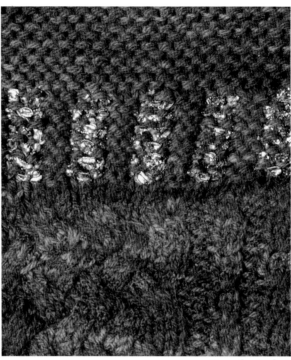

Sampler Jacket

We now know that 32 fits into 76 two times. Multiply 32 x 2 = 64 stitches. Next find out how many extra stitches we have by subtracting 64 from 76 = 12 extra stitches. Place half of the extra stitches before and half after your shaping as follows: K6 (Inc 1, K1) K6 for an increase, and K6 (K2tog) K6 for a decrease. In case of an odd number of extra stitches, place 1 extra stitch at the end. The number of stitches used in parentheses equals 2, which will be increased or decreased 32 times. For your pattern, adjust the number of stitches in parentheses to match the number your division will produce.

Openwork Pullover

LASSO TECHNIQUE

The following patterns use this technique: Poncho with Sleeves, Diagonal Poncho, Ruffle Capelet, Domino Shawl, Backdrop Pullover, and Openwork Pullover.

Join a new strand of yarn by tying it to the old tail using the lasso knot. Make a large slipknot just as you do when casting on. Take the old tail (or ball of yarn, if uncut) through the slipknot.

Pull the tail of the old yarn and the new until the slipknot rides up to the needle and closes shut. To begin knitting, hold the short tails in your left hand to keep the slipknot from sliding down, then insert the needle and continue working.

This knot is easy to use and small enough to leave in the fabric before weaving the tails in the end.

Always leave at least a 6" (15cm) tail of both yarns and tie in where necessary. You do not always have to plan where to start. Keep in mind that if there is a knot, you should cut the yarn and join again. Finally, take your large tapestry needle, and carefully weave in the ends on the wrong side.

SLIPPED STITCHES

The following patterns use this technique: Openwork Pullover, Sampler Jacket, Vintage Purse, Felted Messenger Tote, and Felted Jazz Bag.

A slipped stitch is a stitch moved from the LH needle to the RH needle without working the yarn through it. The yarn will be passing the stitch either in the front or the back depending on your pattern. When the instructions simply state "Slip st", slip the stitch purlwise to avoid twisting the stitch, (picture 1).

1.

Slip stitches knitwise (picture 2) when instructed in the pattern or while decreasing such as: SKP (Slip, knit, pass) and SSK (Slip, slip, knit).

2.

FELTING WOOL

The following patterns use this technique: Felted Messenger Tote, and Felted Jazz Bag.

To make a sturdy felt design, first knit the shape, bind off all stitches and weave in the ends. Next, wash the item using hot water, mild soap, and agitation to shrink it down. Follow these simple steps: Place bound off knitting inside a zipper pillowcase along with some jeans or heavy towels. Select hot water, low level, add a teaspoon of Eucalan® or other mild wool detergent, and start wash cycle. Stand by until wash cycle has completed and drum has emptied. Open to check felting: It is done when the knit stitches are no longer visible. If needed, run the hot wash again. Rinse if necessary, but do not spin! Spinning can set a permanent crease in the felted fabric. Lay flat or drape over a box to air dry.

BRIDGING FELT WITH KNITTING

The following patterns use this technique: Felted Messenger Tote, and Felted Jazz Bag.

For a special contrast, we sometimes like to add a soft knit piece to a sturdy felted fabric. Before felting, change to colorfast waste cotton in a thinner gauge and work 1 row. Bind off and tie cotton tails together. Proceed with Felting Wool instructions (opposite side). With right side facing, pick up stitches at the base of the first row of waste cotton by drawing loops through using a small crochet hook, (picture 1). Transfer stitches

1.

onto knitting needle, (picture 2). Cut bind off corner of waste cotton and unravel all the cotton. Proceed with the knitting instructions.

2.

3-NEEDLE BIND OFF

The following patterns use this technique: Faraoese Shawl, Chameleon Sweater, Long Chenille Vest, Backdrop Pullover, Felted Messenger Tote, Felted Jazz Bag, and Fur Loop Bag.

Knitters love to knit more than they love to sew. At certain times you can knit seams together using a 3-needle bind off by joining the two fabrics together and binding off at the same time. This technique is commonly used for shoulder seams, or any time we are joining the same

2.

1.

number of stitches from two needles. This is easy to do and produces a perfect seam, especially important in visible areas such as a shoulder.

First, bring the right sides together and hold each needle with stitches to be bound off in your left hand. In your right hand, work with a

third needle. Knit stitches on both needles together (picture 1), and bind off at the same time (picture 2).

Turn the fabric over and you have a perfectly lined up seam (picture 3).

3.

CROCHET SEAMS

The following patterns use this technique: Template Poncho, Shaped Fur Poncho, Ruana Stash Poncho, Diagonal Poncho, Chameleon Sweater, Cuddly Pullover, Long Chenille Vest, Dressy Yoke Top, Openwork Pullover, and Sampler Jacket.

Even if you do not crochet, I recommend having a few crochet hooks to finish off the seams. Most knitters are not fond of sewing seams and some yarns can present a real challenge. The solution is crocheting the seams together. The crochet seam can be pulled out easily if it's not turning out well. Also, there is less chance of splitting yarn when using a crochet hook. Finally, a crocheted seam adds stability to an otherwise stretchy fabric, and may save a project. Give it a try and compare the results. With right sides together, bring crochet hook through first stitch in the corner of both layers (picture 1).

1.

Note: For an even seam, always insert the hook behind one full stitch on either side (you will see 4 strands on the hook).

2.

Holding the yarn over your left index finger, (picture 2) move hook under the yarn to catch it and pull the yarn through both fabrics and the stitch on the hook until 1 new stitch remains. Repeat in the second stitch of both layers and continue working across the seam, checking that both layers match. I recommended using large knitter's pins to hold the layers together, especially if the fabric is a bit stretchy or curls under as a result of the stockinette stitch pattern. I am frequently asked, "Should I use the same yarn for the seam?" If using a textured yarn, the answer is "Yes, as long as you are crocheting the seams you won't have a problem, and the yarn will blend perfectly." Choose a crochet hook one size smaller than the needles used to knit the garment. To convert from knitting to crocheting, match the mm sizes on the needles with the mm sizes on the crochet hook.

PICKING UP STITCHES

The following patterns use this technique: Template Poncho, Shaped Fur Poncho, Poncho with Sleeves, Mink Fur Cape, Faraoese Shawl, Domino Shawl, Chameleon Sweater, Cuddly Pullover, Dressy Cape, Openwork Pullover, Sampler Jacket, Vintage Purse, Felted Messenger Tote, and Felted Jazz Bag.

Basic knitting skills include picking up stitches along the knitted edge of a fabric. This is done when finishing a neckband, adding a hem, or knitting a bag with a bottom. To facilitate the process, use a smaller needle or a crochet hook to draw the stitches through the fabric. With the right side facing, insert the needle, front to back, under the first stitch on the edge of the fabric. Wrap the yarn around the needle and pull it through. Continue in the next or every other space depending on the number of stitches in the pattern. To see the spaces clearly, stretch the fabric with your left hand pulling it to the left. Working across, stitches are separated by two strands in the fabric. Working along the side, rows are separated by one strand in the fabric. Place stitch markers on the needle to help keep track of how many stitches have been picked up on different sections of the project. This will balance the number of stitches on either side. If you are having difficulty picking up the exact number of stitches in the pattern, don't panic. It is always better to pick up too many stitches initially than too few as this may cause holes in the fabric.

Count the number of stitches you have picked up, compare it to the pattern, and work one adjustment row by increasing or decreasing evenly to match the number of stitches in the pattern. If your fabric is very stretchy, you may want to pick up twisted stitches, as this will produce a more secure seam. Simply throw the yarn around the needle in the opposite direction over the top of the needle. If all else fails, it is easy to pull out the stitches and start over.

SELF-MADE BUTTONS

The following patterns use this technique: Mink Fur Cape and Felted Jazz Bag.

Use a small plastic ring and single crochet tightly around the entire ring. Join round with a slipstitch. Work another round of single crochet around the ring and wrap over the first round. Join round with a slipstitch. Cut yarn leaving an 8" (20cm) tail and pull through last stitch to bind off. Thread tapestry needle with yarn tail and pick up the outside loop from every single crochet. Gather them together and pull the strand to the back. Tie ends together.

BUTTON LOOP

The following patterns use this technique: Mink Fur Cape, Dressy Cape, and Felted Jazz Bag.

Using a small crochet hook, make a chain long enough to wrap around button from the opposite side. Turn and work slip stitches into the chain. Cut yarn and bind off. Sew loop ends to opposite side of button.

1.

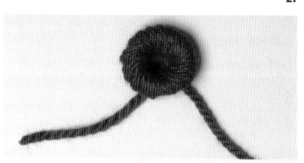

2.

3.

Felted Jazz Bag

Template Poncho

This is the easiest and most versatile poncho pattern available. Knit in two identical rectangles, this template pattern offers a choice of four sizes in four gauges with a variety of yarns. A simple chart shows how many stitches to cast on, and how long to knit the panels. You can also find how many yards to purchase for the panels, and how many are needed for the stylish fur border. Illustrated step-by-step instructions take you through the finishing.

YARN (as shown on model)
 7 balls Plymouth Alpaca Bouclé *70yds (63m) 50g (90% alpaca, 10% nylon) Color: #3676* trimmed with 1 ball Crystal Palace Whisper *97yds (87m) 50g (100% micro fiber nylon) Color: #9268*

 3 balls Plymouth Combolo *47yds (42m) 50g (66% nylon, 30% tactel, 4% polyester) Color: #1038*

NEEDLES (as shown on model)
 US #11 (8mm) or size needed to obtain gauge.

GAUGE (as shown on model)
 In Garter Stitch pattern 2.5 sts = 1" (2.5cm).

SIZE (as shown on model)
 Small

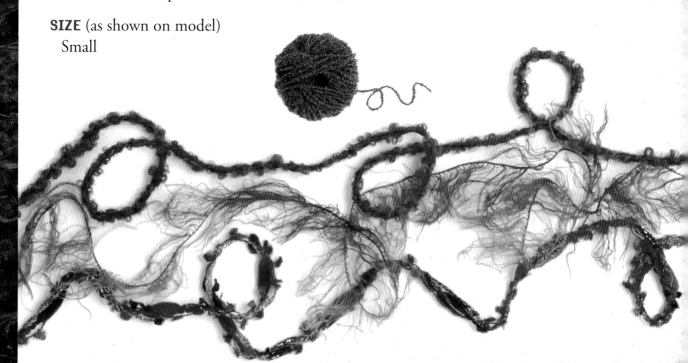

TEMPLATE PONCHO

TO FIT	SMALL	MEDIUM	LARGE	1X
Gauge: 2 sts = 1" + Fur Trim	CO 36 sts Length 28" (71cm) Total yds 388 + 85	CO 38 sts Length 29" (73.5cm) Total yds 420 + 90	CO on 40 sts Length 30" (76cm) Total yds 475 + 95	CO on 44 sts Length 32" (81cm) Total yds 555 + 100
Gauge: 2.5 sts = 1" + Fur Trim	CO 45 sts Length 28" (71cm) Total yds 464 +95	CO 48 sts Length 29" (73.5cm) Total yds 506 + 100	CO on 50 sts Length 30" (76cm) Total yds 568 + 105	CO on 55 sts Length 32" (81cm) Total yds 664 + 115
Gauge: 3 sts = 1" + Fur Trim	CO 54 sts Length 28" (71cm) Total yds 490 + 105	CO 57 sts Length 29" (73.5cm) Total yds 534 + 110	CO on 60 sts Length 30" (76cm) Total yds 600 + 120	CO on 66 sts Length 32" (81cm) Total yds 700 + 130
Gauge: 4 sts = 1" + Fur Trim	CO 72 sts Length 28" (71cm) Total yds 690 + 125	CO 76 sts Length 29" (73.5cm) Total yds 754 + 130	CO on 80 sts Length 30" (76cm) Total yds 847 + 140	CO on 88 sts Length 32" (81cm) Total yds 900 + 150

FRONT AND BACK (make two)

CO number of sts from chart for your size and gauge!

Please knit a swatch and read your stitch gauge carefully! Work even until piece measures length in chart. Knit in your desired stitch pattern complementing your choice of yarn! e.g. Smooth solid color yarn, use a seed stitch. Alternatively, textured yarn, knit in garter stitch.

HELPFUL HINT

Before binding off, measure the rectangle and make sure it is 10" (25cm) longer than wide to allow for the neck opening.

FINISHING

Step 1: RS tog crochet seam (p.21) as shown leaving 10" (25cm) opening for neck.

Step 2: RS facing fold long side over to meet at corner as shown.

Step 3: Fold short end over to meet, and crochet other seam as shown WS facing.

FUR TRIM

Worked in Reverse Stockinette st. Right side facing, pick up and knit (p.22) sts in every other st from seam to seam making sure to pick up 1 st in the corner.

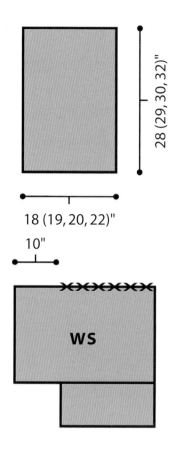

28 (29, 30, 32)"

18 (19, 20, 22)"

10"

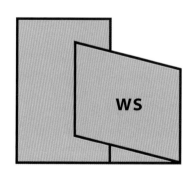

WS

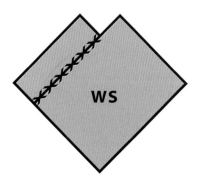

WS

WS

Next row: (WS) Knit to corner, inc 1, pm (p.13), knit 1, pm, inc 1, knit to end.

Next row: (RS) Purl. Repeat last two rows. Bind off loosely. Repeat on other half of poncho from seam to seam. Weave in ends and join fur trim sides together.

TECHNIQUES

Working with Stitch Markers (p.13)

Crochet Seams (p.21)

Picking Up Stitches (p.22)

Shaped Fur Poncho

This lightweight, soft and fluffy poncho goes everywhere. The stylish poncho is worked on large needles in two pieces of Stockinette stitch holding three different yarns together—a bouclé and two fur yarns. Slightly shaped shoulders offer a comfortable fit with a crew neck. Great for a cool evening walk on the boardwalk.

YARN

7 balls Plymouth Alpaca Bouclé *70yds (63m) 50g (90% alpaca, 10% nylon) Color: #2028*

3 balls Trendsetter Voila Print *208yds (187m) 50g (100% nylon) Color: #19*

4 balls Trendsetter Aura *148yds (133m) 50g (100% nylon) Color: #19*

NEEDLES

US #19 (15mm) 29" (73.5cm) circular and US #15 (10mm) 16" (40.5cm) or size needed to obtain gauge.

GAUGE

In Stockinette Stitch pattern 6 sts and 10 rows = 4" (10cm) using US #19 needles and 3 strands held tog.

SIZE

One size fits all.

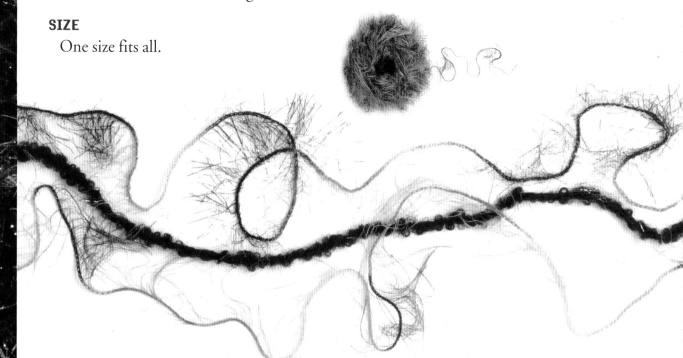

SHAPED FUR PONCHO

BACK

Cast on 3 sts.

Row 1: (WS): Purl

Row 2: (RS): K1, M1, place marker (p.22), K1, M1, K1 = 5 sts

Row 3: (WS): Purl

Row 4: (RS): K1, K to marker, M1, pass marker (p.22), K1, M1, K to end.

Repeat last two rows always increasing on the right side row until you have 51sts (p.14). Purl 1 row.

BEGIN SHAPING SHOULDERS

Row 50: (RS) K1, SKP, K to marker, M1, pass marker, K1, M1,

K to last 3 sts, K2tog, K1.

Row 51: (WS) Purl.

Row 52: (RS) K to marker, M1, pass marker, K1, M1, K to end.

Row 53: (WS) Purl.

Repeat last four rows two more times = 57 sts.

(RS) K23 sts, place on st holder, bind off 11 sts for neck, K 23 sts and place on st holder.

FRONT

Work as for back until shoulder shaping *.

Work rows 50–53 once = 53 sts.

Divide for neck:

(RS) K25, bind off 3, K25.

RIGHT SHOULDER

(WS) P25

(RS) K2tog, knit to end.

Repeat last two rows = 23 sts.

Work two rows Stockinette st.

Transfer sts from Back onto separate needle and join shoulders RS tog working 3-needle bind off (p.20). (Tail is by the neck).

LEFT SHOULDER

(WS) Join yarn at neck and purl row.

(RS) K to last 2 sts, K2tog.

Repeat last two rows = 23 sts.

Work 3 rows Stockinette st.

Transfer sts from Back onto separate needle and join shoulders RS tog working 3-needle bind off (p.20). (Tail is by the neck).

FINISHING

Back: RS facing pick up and knit (p.22) sts 120 sts evenly (in every st) from one shoulder seam to the other shoulder seam using Alpaca Bouclé and US #15, 29" circular needles. Turn and purl one row. Turn and bind off. Repeat on the front. Weave in tails and stitch open edges tog at the same time.

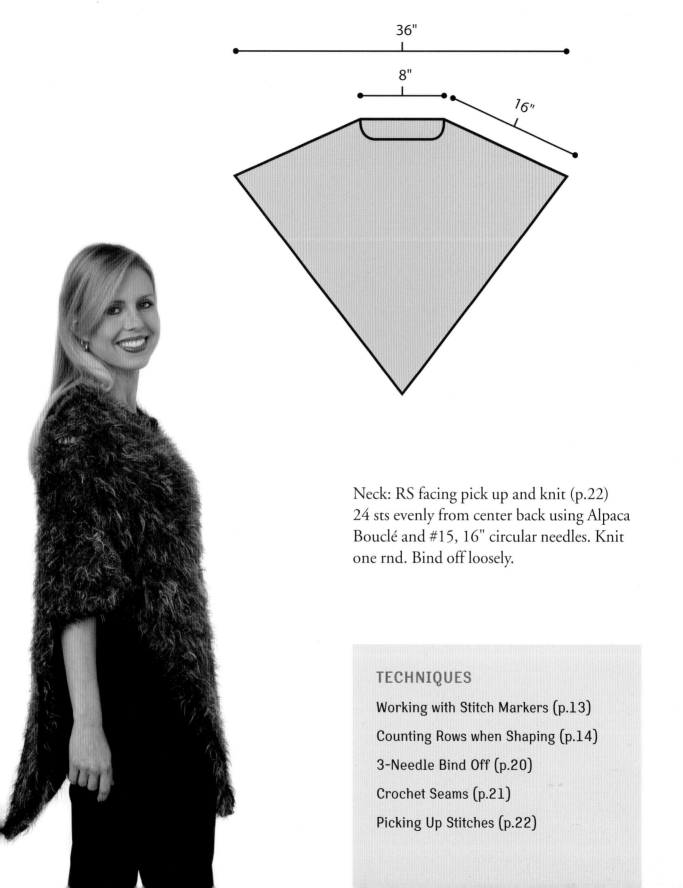

Neck: RS facing pick up and knit (p.22)
24 sts evenly from center back using Alpaca
Bouclé and #15, 16" circular needles. Knit
one rnd. Bind off loosely.

TECHNIQUES

Working with Stitch Markers (p.13)

Counting Rows when Shaping (p.14)

3-Needle Bind Off (p.20)

Crochet Seams (p.21)

Picking Up Stitches (p.22)

Poncho with Sleeves

This multi-colored, comfortable poncho showcases an array of synthetic and natural complementary yarns. Combine the feel of a relaxed poncho with practical sleeves for a smart look to take anywhere. Knit in a basic Garter stitch with stripes of color and built in fringe, this cozy, warm poncho features an oversized polo neck for added style and comfort.

YARN

3 (3) balls Trendsetter Checkmate *70yds (67m) 50g (100% nylon) Color: #1037*

3 (3) balls Berroco Suede *120yds (111m) 50g (100% nylon) Color:#3714*

2 (2) balls Crystal Palace Fizz *120yds (111m) 50g (100% polyester) Color: #9152*

2 (3) balls Needful San Mateo *88yds (80m) 50g (60% nylon, 40% tactel MF) Color: #4182*

1 (2) balls Rowan Felted Tweed *191yds (175m) 50g (50% merino wool, 25% alpaca, 25% viscose) Color: #133*

2 (3) balls Berroco Jewel FX *57yds (52m) 25g (94% rayon, 6% metallic) Color: #6904*

3 (3) balls Naturally Woodland *111yds (100m) 50g (77% mohair, 14% acrylic, 5% nylon, 4% polyester) Color: #02*

2 (2) balls Crystal Palace Cotton Chenille *98yds (88m) 50g (100% cotton) Color: #8166*

1 (2) balls Needful Sinflex Tactel *166yds (150m) 20g (60% tactel, 40% sinflex) Color: #001*

2 (3) balls Trendsetter Dune *90yds (81m) 50g (41% mohair, 30% acrylic, 12% viscose, 11% nylon, 6% metal) Color: #70*

NEEDLES

US #10 (6mm) 29" (73.5cm) circular needles or size needed to obtain gauge.

GAUGE

In Garter Stitch pattern 14 sts and 24 rows = 4" (10cm).

SIZES

S/M (L/XL)

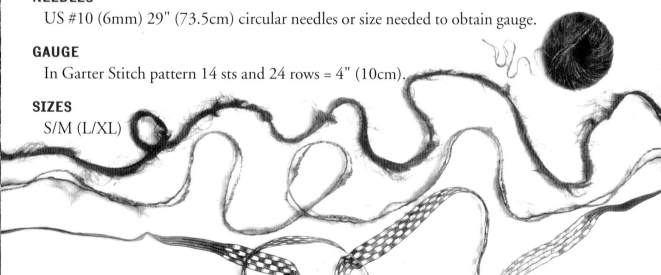

PONCHO WITH SLEEVES

YARN COLOR SEQUENCE

1. Checkmate

2. Suede + Fizz 1 strand of each yarn held tog (4 rows)

3. San Mateo

4. Felted Tweed + Jewel FX 1 strand of each yarn held tog

5. Woodland (4 rows)

6. Cotton Chenille + Sinflex 1 strand of each yarn held tog

7. Dune

Work in Garter st 2 rows of each color except color 2 and 5, work 4 rows leaving a 5" (12.5cm) tail at the beg and end of each color change.

Note: Always change color on a right side row!

SLEEVE AND BODY (one piece)

Starting with the sleeve, cast on 60 (66) sts. Work even in yarn color pattern for 8" (20cm). Continue inc 1 st at the beg and end of every 4th row until 74 (80) sts. Continue inc 1 st at the beg and end of every other row until 102 (108) sts. Cast on 21 sts at the beg of next two rows for body = 144 (150) sts. Continue inc 1 st at beg and end of every other row until 174 (180) sts. Work even for 6 (18) rows.

SHAPE BACK NECK

Next row: K85 (88), Bind off 4 sts, K85 (88). Continue working on backside of the poncho purling every row, which places the color changes by the hem. Next bind off 1 st

at neck edge 3 more times. Work even for 36 rows. Continue casting on 1 st at neck edge 3 times. Cut yarn.

SHAPE FRONT NECK

Join yarn by neck on front of poncho keeping with color sequence and continue to knit every row. Bind off 1 st at neck edge (beg of row) 3 more times. Work even for 36 (48) rows. Continue casting on 1 st at neck edge (beg of row) 3 times.

BODY AND SLEEVE

Next row knit across both sides to join and work even for 6 (18) rows. Begin decreasing: K2tog at beg and end of every other row until 144 (150) sts. Bind off 21 sts at the beg of next two rows for body = 102 (108) sts.

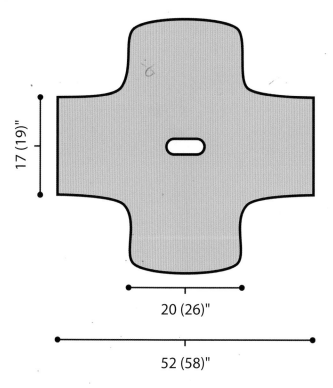

17 (19)"

20 (26)"

52 (58)"

FINISHING SLEEVES

Right side facing, starting by the wrist, pull ends through other layer and tie together as fringe up the seam. Stop before the armhole, leaving the body open. Tie ends into fringe along hem of poncho. Add fringe in missing areas holding 10" (25cm) lengths of 4 different yarns tog.

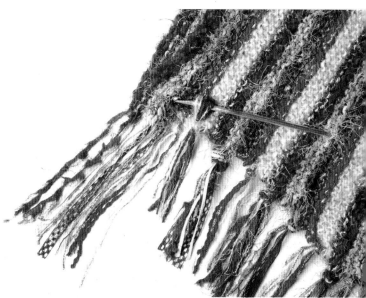

Continue K2tog at beg and end of every other row until 74 (80) sts. Continue K2tog at beg and end of every 4th row until 60 (66) sts. Work even in pattern for 8" (20cm). Bind off loosely.

FINISHING NECK

Weave in any loose ends by neck. Pick up stitches (p.22) and knit around the neck using Dune and US #10 needles = 75 (91) sts overlapping two sts at the join. Work in rib: K1 (P1, K1). Repeat following color sequence leaving 5" (12.5cm) tails at each color change. Work in rib pattern for 2" (5cm). Next row increase evenly to 114 (136) sts. Cont in rib: K1 (P2, K2) K1 until collar measures 6" (15cm). Bind off in rib. Join collar seam by tying fringe through both sides.

TECHNIQUES

Cable Cast On (p.10)

Counting Rows when Shaping (p.14)

Picking Up Stitches (p.22)

Ruana Stash Poncho

Create your own stash yarn by tying together different strands alternating textures, colors, and fibers for a one-of-a-kind yarn. Knit two easy Garter stitch panels worked in diagonal rows by increasing on one end and decreasing on the other end. Wear this masterpiece as a Ruana over your shoulders and tie it together with ribbons wrapped around one big button. Knit one for Fall and one for Spring. Blend new yarns with basic yarns, and pull odd ends from your personal yarn stash.

YARNS

1 ball Plymouth Alpaca Bouclé *70yds (65m) 50g (90% alpaca, 10% nylon) Color: #3676*

1 ball Plymouth Alpaca Bouclé *70yds (65m) 50g (90% alpaca, 10% nylon) Color: #2028*

1 ball Plassard Flore *100yds (92m) 50g (75% kid mohair, 20% wool, 5% nylon) Color: #26*

1 ball Trendsetter Aura Antique *148yds (136m) 50g (100% nylon) Color: #3010*

1 ball King Modigliani *71yds (65m) 50g (100% merino virgin wool) Color: #23*

1 ball Crystal Palace Shimmer *90yds (83m) 50g (86% acrylic, 14% nylon) Color: #1743*

1 ball Plymouth Furlauro *82yds (75m) 50g (100% nylon) Color: #830*

1 ball Crystal Palace Whisper *97yds (90m) 50g (100% micro fiber nylon) Color: #9268*

1 ball Trendsetter Aquarius *96yds (89m) 50g (78% nylon, 22% cotton) Color: #8147*

1 ball Gerifil Banderas *277yds (256m) 50g (100% nylon) Color: #117*

1 ball Plymouth Flirt *93 yds (86m) 50g (100% nylon) Color: #31*

1 ball Plymouth 24K *187yds (173m) 50g (82% nylon 18% lamé) Color: #1373*

1 ball Needful Capri *104yds (96m) 50g (78% nylon, 22% cotton) Color: #4125*

1 ball Crystal Palace Squiggle *100yds (92m) 50g (50% nylon, 50% polyester) Color: #9211*

1 ball Plymouth Dazzlelash *220 yds (203m) 50g (78% polyester, 22% rayon) Color: #102*

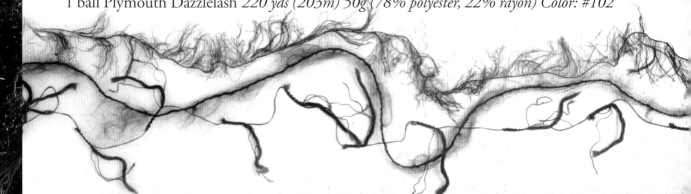

1 hank Berroco Quest *82yds (76m) 50g (100% nylon) Color: #9813*

1 hank Berroco Denim Silk *105 yds (97m) 50g (80% rayon, 20% silk) Color: #1429*

1 hank Crystal Palace Cotton Chenille *98yds (90m) 50g (100% cotton) Color: #3387*

1 ball Trendsetter Joy *65yds (60m) 25g (75% polyamide, 25% polyester) Color: #603*

1 ball Plassard Neptune *43yds (40m) 50g (65% wool, 35% polyamide) Color: #003*

1 ball Crystal Palace Glam *87yds (80m) 50g (36% acrylic, 35% rayon, 15% wool, 14% nylon) Color: #2136*

1 ball Rowan Yorkshire Tweed Chunky *109 yds (101m) 100g (100% pure new wool) Color: #553*

1 yd Hanah Silk *1" (2.54cm) wide silk ribbon. Color: Tuscany*

NEEDLES
US #17 (12.75mm) or size needed to obtain gauge.

GAUGE
In Garter Stitch pattern 8 sts and 12 rows = 4" (10cm).

SIZES
S/M (L/XL)

RUANA STASH PONCHO

MAKE GAUGE COORDINATED STASH YARN
Choose a bulky yarn as a guide that knits to gauge worked solo. In the model, the guide yarn is Neptune. Grab several strands of coordinating thinner yarns and hold them tog. With the combination yarns in one hand and the guide strand in the other, loop the two around each other and twist the ends between your fingers until taut. Run your fingers along the join to feel whether the yarns measure the same thickness. Continue to add or subtract strands until you find a matching weight. Holding multiple strands tog, measure 6 arm lengths of your first yarns. Cut yarns. Look for second yarn combination testing the gauge as before. Tie the two yarn combinations tog with an overhand knot.

When choosing yarns, consider working with different yarns alternating textures, colors, and fiber properties. Blend yarns by fiber content; choose a yarn that is at least 50% wool for every third combination to ensure proper strength, as wool retains its shape. Blend yarns by texture; alternate furry yarns with smooth shiny ribbons, nubby yarn, sparkly metallic, and basic yarns. Blend yarns by color; change color combinations each time, using high contrast colors less, but evenly throughout. Using your stash yarn, cast on 40 (48) sts.

PANEL 1
Row 1: (WS): Knit.

Row 2: (RS): K1, Inc 1, K to last 3 sts, K2tog, K1. Place marker (p.13) to remind you that this is the right side row. Repeat last two rows until piece measures 58 (62)" / 147

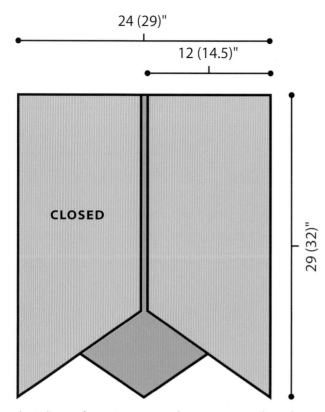

24 (29)"

12 (14.5)"

CLOSED

29 (32)"

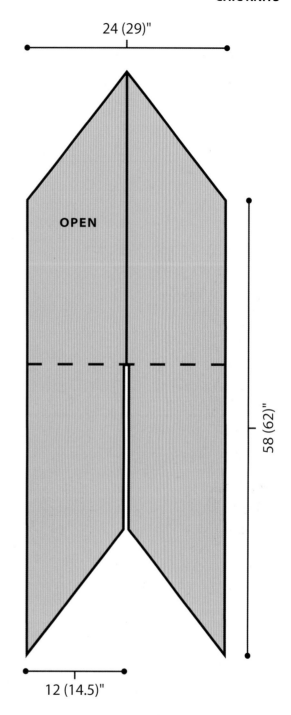

24 (29)"

OPEN

58 (62)"

12 (14.5)"

(158)cm changing yarns by tying overhand knots (see photo) and continuing to knit leaving knot ends hanging on right side of fabric.

PANEL 2

Row 1: (WS): Knit.

Row 2: (RS): K1, K2tog, K to last 2 sts, Inc 1, K1. Place marker (p.13) to remind you that this is the right side row. Repeat last two rows until piece measures same as panel 1, changing yarns by tying overhand knots and continuing to knit leaving knot ends hanging on right side of fabric.

FINISHING

Crochet back seam. Attach big button on left front, and 18" (46cm) long ribbon fringe on right front using 1 strand each silk ribbon, Aquarius, Capri and Shimmer. Wrap fringe around button to close.

TECHNIQUES

Crochet Seams (p.21)

Diagonal Poncho

Achieve a great slimming look with a simple, trouble-free pattern. Knit two squares in diagonal rows from point to point. Increase on the first half and decrease on the second half. The design is in your choice of yarns with shiny hand-dyed rayons, in contrast with darker matte yarns worked in two row repeats leaving a built-in fringe. A cool flip collar can be pinned in place with a stylish brooch. Perfect for cool summer evenings or chilly autumn nights.

YARN AND COLOR SEQUENCE

A: 1 hank Blue Heron Bulky Rayon Chenille *250yds (230m) 8oz (100% rayon) Color: #711 Indigo Sea*

B: 2 hanks Manos del Uruguay Wool *138yds (126m) 100g (100% pure wool) Color: #55*

C: 1 hank Blue Heron Rayon Bouclé *212yds (196m) 8oz (100% rayon) Color: #711 Indigo Sea*

D: 3 balls Needful San Mateo *88yds (80m) 50g (60% nylon, 40% tactel MF) Color: #4178*

E: 1 hank Blue Heron Cotton and Rayon Seed *490yds (452m) 8oz (50% cotton, 50% rayon) Color: #711 Indigo Sea*

NEEDLES

US #9 (5.5mm) 24" (61cm) circular or size needed to obtain gauge.

GAUGE

In Garter Stitch pattern 14 sts and 20 rows = 4" (10cm).

SIZE

One size fits all.

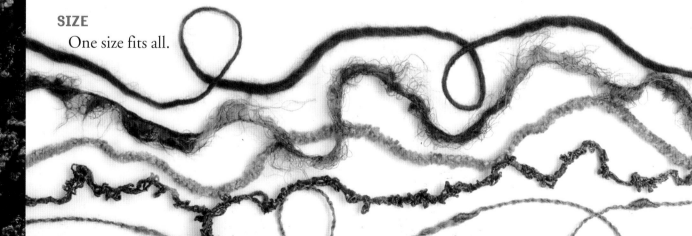

DIAGONAL PONCHO

BACK & FRONT (make two)
With A, cast on 2 sts leaving an 8"
(20cm) tail.
Next row: K1, Inc 1.
Next row: K1, Inc 1, K1. Cut A
leaving an 8" (20cm) tail.

Change to B using the lasso
technique (p.18) leaving an
8" (20cm) tail. K1, Inc 1, K
to end. Repeat last row
once.

Change to C and
continue in the same
manner working 2
rows of each color
following the
color sequence
A thru E.
Always leave
an 8" (20cm)
tail at the
beginning
and end of
a color.

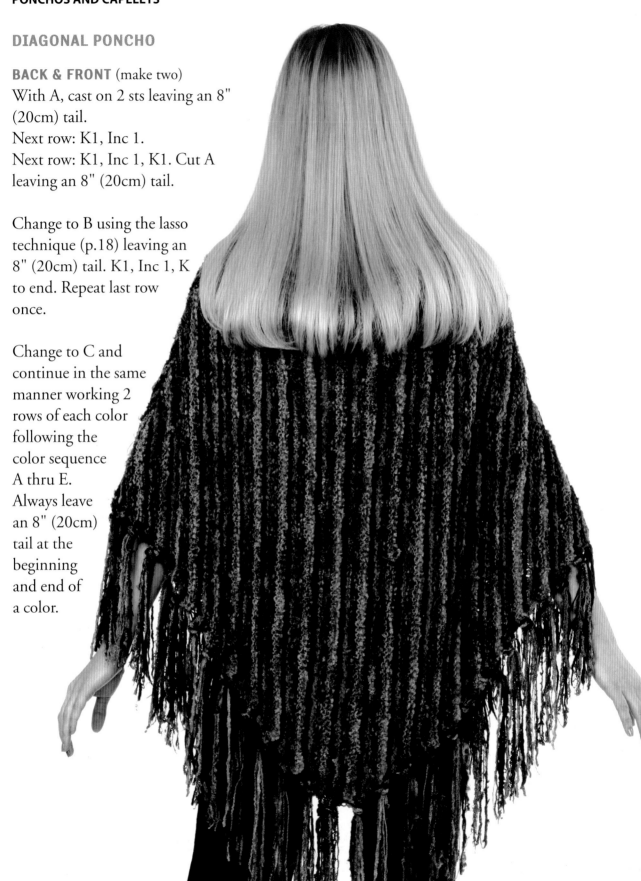

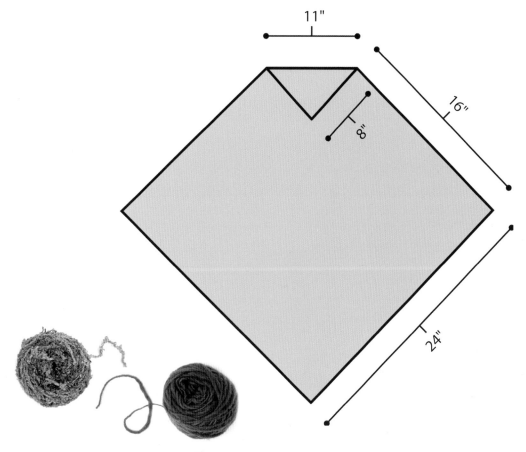

Work until square measures 24" (61cm) along one side and you have 120 sts. Begin decreasing: K1, K2tog, K to end. Repeat until 2 sts remain. Bind off.

FINISHING

(WS) facing, slip crochet stitch (p.21) 16" (40.5cm) sides leaving an 8" (20cm) opening for the neck. Grab 8 tails tog and tie into fringe along hem. Lay over table and cut fringes evenly. Fold neck flap to the outside and optionally pin into place.

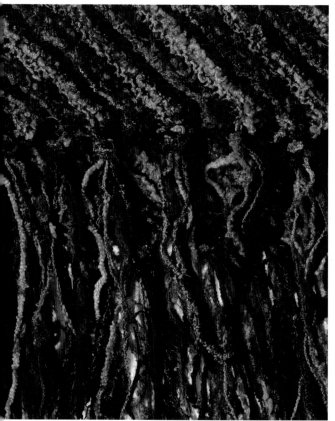

TECHNIQUES

Lasso Technique (p.18)

Crochet Seams (p.21)

Ruffle Capelet

Be the hit of the party with this new vintage flair in frosted ruffles over a marbleized capelet. Knits up quickly in the round on circular needles with mohair, silk, and wool yarns. Make ruffles separately and join to body by knitting them together. The body under the ruffles is ribbed for comfort and the top is shaped slightly to fit around the shoulders. Ultra chic no matter what the occasion.

YARN

1 ball Rowan Kidsilk Haze *229yds (210m) 25g (70% super kid mohair, 30% silk) Color: #604*

1 ball Rowan Kidsilk Haze *229yds (210m) 25g (70% super kid mohair, 30% silk) Color: #590*

1 ball Needful Sinflex Tactel *166yds (150m) 20g (60% tactel, 40% sinflex) Color: #003*

2 hanks Manos del Uruguay Wool *138yds (126m) 100g (100% pure wool) Color: #25*

NEEDLES

US #8 (5mm), US #9 (5.5mm), and US #10.5 (6.5mm) circular needles 29"(73.5cm) long or size needed to obtain gauge.

GAUGE

In Stockinette Stitch pattern 13 sts and 19 rows = 4" (10cm) using 1 strand of Uruguay Wool and US #10.5 needles.

SIZES

Fits chest sizes 37–44" (94–112)cm.

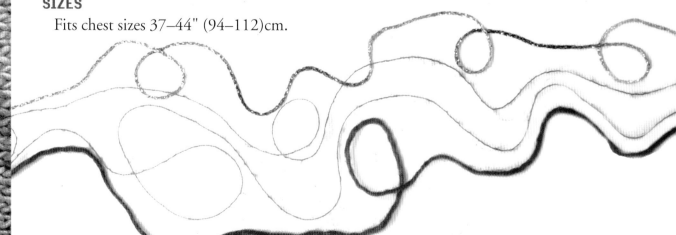

Mink Fur Cape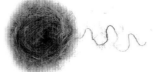

Enjoy making this stylish faux fur cape to snuggle over your shoulders for year round wear in your choice of yarns. Add a simple short row technique to your knitting repertoire for a rectangle that turns on an angle, and fits perfectly around the shoulders. This is a simple pattern that repeats alternating yarn combinations for an elegant mink fur look.

YARN

2 (2) balls Plymouth Royal Cashmere *154yds (142m) 50g (100% cashmere) Color: #1632*

2 (3) balls Lincatex Gold Rush *110yds (102m) 25g (80% rayon, 20% metallised polyester) Color: #92*

2 (2) balls Trendsetter Voila Print *208yds (192m) 50g (100% nylon) Color: #11*

4 (6) balls Adriafil Stars *72yds (66m) 50g (50% viscose, 50% nylon) Color: #89*

NEEDLES

US #8 (5mm) 16–24" (40.5–61cm) circular and US #9 (5.5mm) long single pointed or circular 24" (61cm) needles or size needed to obtain gauge.

GAUGE

In Stockinette Stitch pattern 17 sts and 22 rows = 4" (10cm) using US #9 (5.5mm) needles and 1 strand of Royal Cashmere and Gold Rush held tog.

FINISHED SIZES

Short 12" / 30.5cm (Long 18" / 46cm)

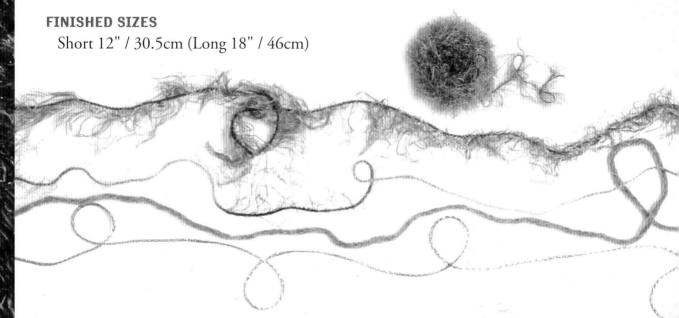

MINK FUR CAPE

Starting at left front with US #9 needles and one strand of Royal Cashmere and Gold Rush held tog, cast on 48 (72) sts. Knit 5 rows.

Change to one strand of Stars and Voila Print held tog:

Row 1: (RS) Purl 28 (52), Wrap & Turn (see below), Knit 28 (52), Turn, Purl entire row.

WRAP & TURN

Also called Short Rows, this simple technique is designed to shape a fabric by working more rows over selected sts on the needle, whereby we stop mid row and turn. To achieve this effect without creating holes in the fabric, wrap the yarn around the neighboring stitch before turning. Work as follows from * to *:

*Slip next st purl wise, pass yarn to opposite side of work (if knitting bring yfwd, if purling move ybk), return slipped st back onto LH needle, TURN *.

Row 2: (WS) Knit.

Row 3: (RS) Purl 38 (62), Wrap & Turn, Knit 38 (62), Turn, Purl entire row.

Row 4: (WS) Knit.

Row 5: (RS) Purl 28 (52), Wrap & Turn, Knit 28 (52), Turn, Purl entire row.

Row 6: (WS) Knit.

Change to 1 strand of Royal Cashmere and Gold Rush held tog:

Row 7: (RS) Knit 38 (62), Wrap & Turn, Purl 38 (62), Turn, Knit entire row.

Row 8: (WS) K1, Purl to last st, K1.

Row 9: (RS) Knit 28 (52), Wrap & Turn, Purl 28 (52), Turn, Knit entire row.

Row 10: (WS) K1, Purl to last st, K1.

Repeat rows 1–10 twelve more times or desired length to fit around the shoulders. Work rows 1–6 once more. Knit 5 rows. Bind off loosely.

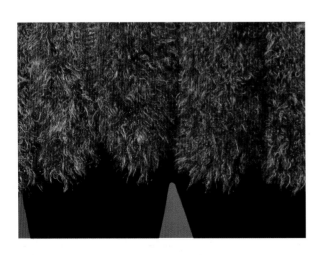

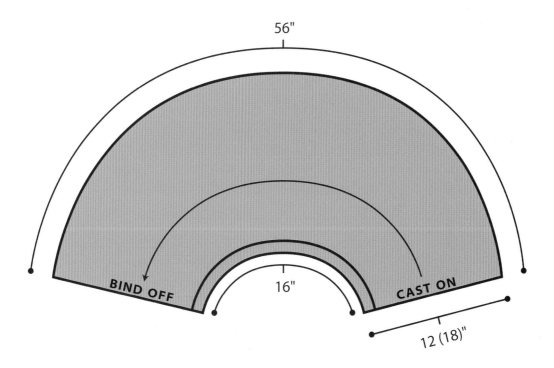

56"

BIND OFF

16"

CAST ON

12 (18)"

NECK
RS facing, pick up (p.22) and knit 72 sts in every other row using US #8 needles and 1 strand of Royal Cashmere and Gold Rush held tog. Knit 5 rows. Bind off.

TECHNIQUES
Picking Up Stitches (p.22)

Self-Made Buttons (p.23)

Domino Shawl

Knit this stunning shawl in simple Garter stitch rows with center row decreases to form an interesting domino pattern. The center back diamond is worked first, and is joined by a half diamond on either side for a triangular shaped shawl. Make it spectacular by working rows of many different textured yarns, choosing either contrasting colors for a bold statement, or subtle ones for a softer look. Finish with a knit fur band.

YARN

A: 2 balls Crystal Palace Merino Frappe *140yds (126m) 50g (80% merino wool, 20% polyamide) Color: #046*

B: 2 balls Plymouth Odyssey Glitz *65yds (58m) 50g (60% nylon, 37% wool, 3% lamé) Color: #900*

C: 2 balls S. Charles Sabrina *60yds (55m) 50g (45% wool, 24% cotton, 16% viscose, 9% acrylic, 6% polyamide) Color: #2*

D: 1 ball Stylecraft Eskimo *98yds (90m) 50g (100% polyester) Color: #5067*

E: 1 ball Trendsetter Checkmate *70yds (67m) 50g (100% nylon) Color: #811*

F: 3 (4) balls Plymouth Combolo *47yds (42m) 50g (66% nylon, 30% tactel, 4% polyester) Color: #1025*

G: 1 ball Crystal Palace Glam *87yds (78m) 50g (36% acrylic, 35% rayon, 15% wool, 14% nylon) Color: #2138*

H: 1 ball Lana Gatto Crystal *87yds (80m) 50g (63% viscose, 20% nylon, 17% polyester) Color: #4116*

I: 1 ball Stylecraft Eskimo *98yds (90m) 50g (100% polyester) Color: #5211*

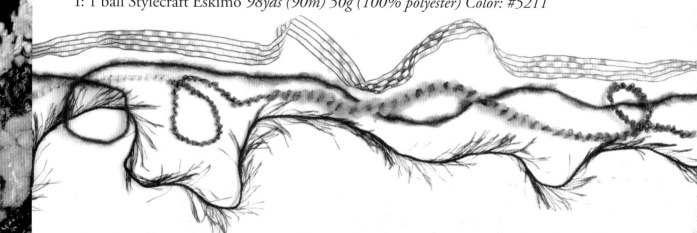

NEEDLES

US #10.5 (6.5mm) and US #11 (8mm) 29"
(60.5cm) circular or size needed to obtain
gauge.

GAUGE

In Garter Stitch pattern 10 sts and 14 rows
= 4" (10cm) following color sequence
using US #11 needles.

SIZES

Short: 30" (76cm) long x 60" (1.53m) wide.
Long: 36" (91cm) long x 72" (1.85m) wide
including fur trim.

DOMINO SHAWL

With A and US #11 needles, knit cast on
(p.10) 100 (122) sts. Set-up row (WS): K49
(60), K2tog tbl and mark this center stitch
with a safety pin, K49 (60), yarn fwd, slip 1,
turn work = 99 (121) sts.

Row 1 (RS): Slip 1, knit to end.

Row 2 (WS): Slip 1, knit to 1 st before the
marked center st, K3tog tbl and move the
marker up to this row, knit to end.

*Note: You will be making a centered double
decrease every WS row. Change colors on the
RS rows using the lasso technique (p.18).*

Repeat rows 1 & 2 following this color
sequence:

2 rows B
2 rows C
2 rows D
2 rows B
2 rows E
4 rows F
2 rows A

4 rows D
2 rows B
2 rows G
4 rows C
2 rows F
4 rows A

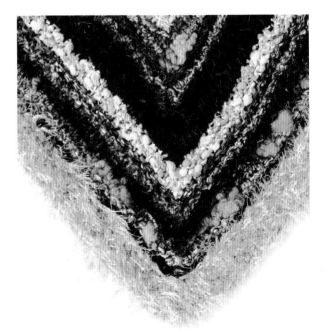

Continue until 5 sts remain.

Next row (RS): Slip 1, K to end.

Next row (WS): Slip 1, K3tog tbl, K1, turn
= 3 sts.

Next row (RS): Slip 1, K2, turn.

Next row (WS): K3tog tbl, cut yarn leaving a
4" (10cm) tail. Fasten off.

RIGHT HAND TRIANGLE

Pick up row: (RS) With A and US #11
needles knit cast on (p.10) 50 (61) sts, then
pick up and knit (p.22) 50 (61) sts along
right side of diamond, turn. Set-up row
(WS) K49 (60), K2tog tbl and mark this
center stitch with a safety pin, K49 (60),
yarn fwd, slip 1, turn work = 99 (121) sts.

Row 1: (RS) Slip 1, SSK, K to last 3 sts,
K2tog, K1.

Faraoese Shawl

This classic favorite returns as a short shawl in a simple Garter stitch pattern, garnished with a knit ruffle, in a supple alpaca ribbon yarn. The Faraoese shawl has a smart shape around the shoulders, which keeps it comfortably in place. A flattering style that is easy to shape using stitch markers on the needles.

YARN

5 balls Plymouth Baby Alpaca DK *125yds (112m) 50g (100% baby alpaca) Color: #207*

1 ball Plymouth Eros *165yds (148m) 50g (100% nylon) Color: #2020*

NEEDLES

US #9 (5.50mm) and US #10.5 (6.50mm) 29" (73.5cm) circular or size needed to obtain gauge.

GAUGE

In Garter Stitch pattern 17 sts and 30 rows = 4" (10cm) using US #9 needles and 1 strand Baby Alpaca DK.

SIZE

One size fits all.

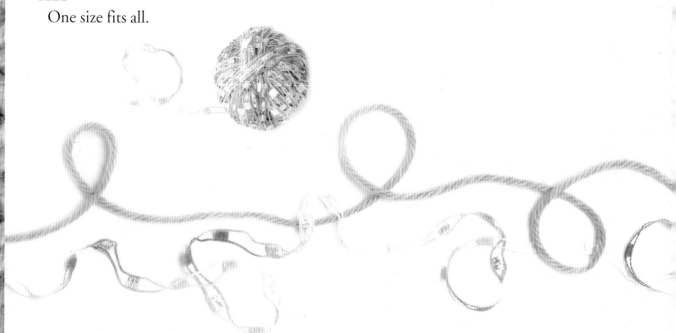

FARAOESE SHAWL

Cast on 305 sts. Set up row (WS): K6, place marker (p.13), K133, place marker, K27, place marker, K133, place marker, K6 (6+133+27+133+6).

Main Row 1: (RS): K6, pm, K2tog, K to end passing markers.

Main Row 2: (WS): K6, pm, K2tog, K to 2 sts before marker, K2tog, pm, K to marker, pm, K2tog, K to marker, pm, K6. Rep last two rows 11 times = 257 sts (6+109+27+109+6). See Counting rows when shaping (p.14).

CENTER BACK GUSSET

Dec Row 1: (RS): K6, pm, K2tog, K to end passing markers.

Dec Row 2: (WS): K6, pm, K2tog, K to 2 sts before marker, K2tog, pm, K2tog, K to 2 sts before marker, K2tog, pm, K2tog, K to marker, pm, K6. = 251 sts (6+107+25+107+6).

Repeat Main Rows 1 & 2 four more times = 235 sts (6+99+25+99+6).

Work Dec Rows 1 & 2 = 229 sts (6+97+23+97+6).

Repeat Main Rows 1 & 2 four more times = 213 sts (6+89+23+89+6). Work Dec Rows 1 & 2 = 207 sts (6+87+21+87+6).

Cont in this manner rep from * to * two more times until 163 sts (6+67+17+67+6). Repeat Main Rows 1 & 2 four more times = 147 sts (6+59+17+59+6).

BEGIN SHAPING SHOULDERS

Shoulder Row 1: (RS): K6, pm, K3 (K5, K2tog) rep 8 times, pm, K2tog, K to 2 sts before marker, K2tog, pm, K3 (K5, K2tog) rep 8 times, pm, K6 = 129 sts (6+51+15+51+6).

Shoulder Row 2: (WS): K6, pm, K2tog, K to last 8 sts passing markers, K2tog, pm, K6 = 127 sts (6+50+15+50+6). Rep Main rows 1 & 2 three times = 115 sts (6+44+15+44+6).

Shoulder Row 3: (RS): K6, pm, (K2, K2tog) rep 11 times, pm, K2tog, K to 2 sts before marker, K2tog, pm, (K2, K2tog) rep 11 times, pm, K6 = 91 sts (6+33+13+33+6).

Shoulder Row 4: (WS): K6, pm, K2tog, K to marker, pm, K13, pm, K to 2 sts before marker, K2tog, pm, K6 = 89 sts (6+32+13+32+6). Rep Main rows 1 & 2 three times = 77 sts (6+26+13+26+6).

Shoulder Row 5: (RS): K6, pm, (K2tog) rep 13 times, pm, K2tog, K to 2 sts before marker, K2tog, pm, (K2tog) rep 13 times, pm, K6 = 49 sts (6+13+11+13+6).

Shoulder Row 6: (WS): K6, pm, K2tog, K to marker, pm, K11, pm, K to 2 sts before marker, K2tog, pm, K6 = 47 sts (6+12+11+12+6).

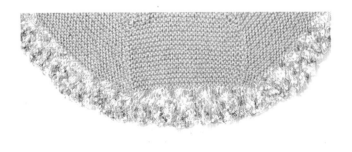

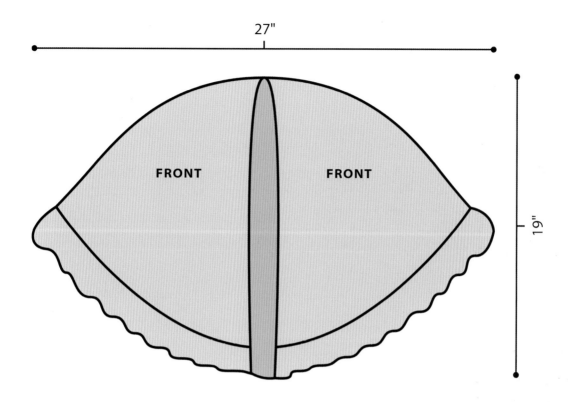

27"

19"

FRONT

FRONT

Next row: (RS): K6, pm, (K2tog, K1), pm, (K2tog, K7, K2tog) pm, (K1, K2tog), pm, K6 = 37 sts (6+8+9+8+6). (WS) K6, pm, K2tog, K to last 8 sts passing markers, K2tog, pm, K6 = 35 sts. (RS) K6, pm, K2tog, K3, K2tog, pm, K2tog, K5, K2tog, pm, K2tog, K3, K2tog, pm, K6 = 29 sts. (WS) K6, pm, K2tog, K to last 8 sts passing markers, K2tog, pm, K6 = 27 sts. (RS) K6, pm, (K2tog) twice, pm, K2tog, K3, K2tog, pm, (K2tog) twice, pm, K6 = 21 sts. (WS) K6, pm, K2tog, pm, K2tog, K1, K2tog, pm, K2tog, pm, K6 = 17 sts. (RS) K4, (K2tog) five times, K3 =12 sts.

(WS) Bind off remaining 12 sts using the 3-needle bind off technique (p.20).

RUFFLE

RS facing, using US #9 needles and 1 strand Plymouth Eros pick up (p.22) and knit 305 sts in every st along cast on edge. Change to US #10.5 needles and knit 4 rows. Next row: Increase in every st = 610 sts. Knit 3 rows. Bind off.

TECHNIQUES

Cable Cast On (p.10)

Working with Stitch Markers (p.13)

Counting Rows when Shaping (p.14)

3-Needle Bind Off (p.20)

Picking Up Stitches (p.22)

Tops and Sweaters

Knit it and wear it in style! Choose from four long sleeve pullovers with various neck styles and yarn combinations. The **Chameleon Sweater** features a silky fur cowl neck that is worn over the shoulders for a chic look. The **Cuddly Pullover** is worked holding a silky fur yarn together with a cotton ribbon throughout and features a big polo neck and matching scarf. If you prefer a V-neck, the **Backdrop Pullover** has a shawl collar knit with alternating novelty yarns held together with a main yarn. Knit the **Openwork Pullover** in a lightweight cotton-linen blend finished with a crew neck, and accent with a sheer ribbon lace yoke and matching ribbon scarf.

The easy-to-knit, **Long Vest** in cotton chenille and alternating accent yarns features a cool stand-up collar and handy pockets. Make a black **Dressy Yoke Top** and **Cape** ensemble in coordinating yarns with a variegated gold trim. The **Dressy Cape** is knit in an easy garter stitch and features beautiful shaped shoulders. You'll love the fur trimmed **Sampler Jacket**, worked in hand-dyed wool and accented with novelty yarns in different stitch patterns throughout. A knitter's delight, this exceptional pattern takes you through with clear, easy-to-follow, row-by-row instructions. These wonderful sweaters and tops are as great to knit as they are to wear!

Chameleon Sweater

Take style to the ultimate edge with this comfortable, eye-catching sweater designed to turn heads and garner compliments. Wear the collar down over the shoulders, or pull it up as a cuddly cowl neck. Stockinette and rib stitches make this an easy knitting experience. The supple nylon fur has the look and soft feel of angora, minus the shedding and high cost.

YARN

4 (5, 5, 6) balls Plymouth Baby Alpaca Grande *110yds (99m) 100g (100% baby alpaca) Color: #2050*

4 (4, 5, 5) balls Needful Santa Ana *66yds (60m) 50g (33% wool, 67% nylon) Color: #4165*

NEEDLES

US #10.5 (6.50mm) 29" (73.5cm) circular and long single pointed needles, and US #11 (8mm) long single pointed needles or size needed to obtain gauge.

GAUGE

In Stockinette Stitch pattern 12 sts and 14 rows = 4" (10cm) with US #11 needles and 1 strand Baby Alpaca Grande.

FINISHED SIZES

Chest 41 (45, 49, 53)" / 104 (114, 124.5, 134.5)cm.

Length 19 (20, 21, 22)" / 48 (51, 53, 56)cm.

Sleeve Length 17 (17.5, 18, 18.5)" / 43 (44.5, 45.5, 47)cm.

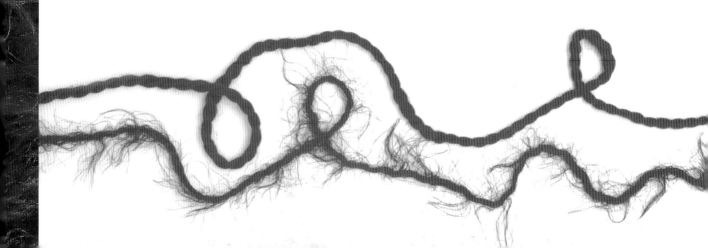

CHAMELEON SWEATER

BACK

With US #10.5 29" circular needles and 1 strand of Santa Ana, cast on 62 (68, 74, 80) sts. Work in K2, P2 rib for 2" (5cm). Change to US #11 needles and 1 strand of Baby Alpaca Grande and cont in St st until piece measures 19 (20, 21, 22)" / 48 (51, 53, 56)cm from beg, place sts on a holder.

FRONT

Work as for back until piece measures 17.5 (18.5, 19.5, 20.5)" / 44.5 (47, 49.5, 52)cm from beg.

FRONT NECK SHAPING

(RS) K15 place rem sts on a holder. (WS) P2tog, P to end.

(RS) K to last 2 sts, K2tog. Rep last two rows until 11 sts. Work even until shoulder measures the same length as the back. Place sts on a holder. RS facing, leave center 32 (38, 44, 50) sts on the holder, and slip 15 shoulder sts back on needle. Join yarn. (RS) K15. (WS) P to last 2 sts, P2tog. (RS) K2tog, K to end.

Rep last two rows until 11 sts. Work even until shoulder measures the same length as the back. Place sts on a holder.

SHOULDER SEAMS

Slip front 11 and back 11 shoulder sts onto separate needles. With RS facing, bind off

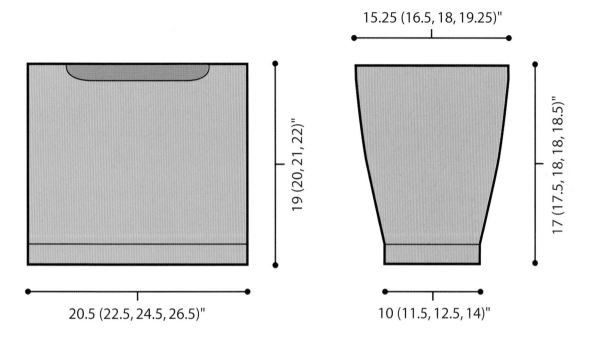

15.25 (16.5, 18, 19.25)"

19 (20, 21, 22)"

20.5 (22.5, 24.5, 26.5)"

17 (17.5, 18, 18, 18.5)"

10 (11.5, 12.5, 14)"

using the 3-needle bind off technique (p.20). Neck sts are still left on holders.

SLEEVES (make two)
With US #10.5 needles and 1 strand of Santa Ana cast on 30 (34, 38, 42) sts. Work K2, P2 rib for 2" (5cm). Change to US #11 needles and 1 strand of Baby Alpaca Grande and work in St st, increasing 1 st at the beg and end of every 6th row until 46 (50, 54, 58) sts. Work even until sleeve measures 17 (17.5, 18, 18.5)" / 43 (44.5, 45.5, 47)cm. Bind off.

COLLAR
Slip back and front neck sts onto US #10.5 29" circular needles. Join 1 strand of Santa Ana and knit 40 (46, 52, 58) sts from back, pick up 6 sts along front slope, knit 32 (38, 44, 50) sts from front, pick up and knit 6 sts (p.22) along front slope = 84 (96, 108, 120) sts. Place a marker, join in the round (p.12), and work one rnd increasing 8 sts evenly. Work in K2, P2 rib for 10". Bind off using a larger needle in rib pattern.

FINISHING
Sew in sleeves evenly from shoulder seams. With WS facing, chain crochet sleeve and side seams. Weave in all ends.

TECHNIQUES
Joining in the Round (p.12)

Picking Up Stitches (p.22)

Blocking (p.24)

Cuddly Pullover and Scarf

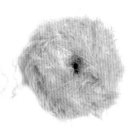

If you can't wear wool, this classic, eye-catching sweater is a silky, ultra-soft blend of lightweight cotton and nylon. The big polo neck drapes beautifully and is fun to pull up and cuddle behind. This three-season sweater uses a Stockinette stitch and can be knit in many comparable yarns. The complementary scarf pattern is playful and features asymmetrical fur yarn at the tips of the scarf.

YARN

7 (8, 8, 9) balls Berroco Zen *110yds (102m) 50g (55% cotton, 45% nylon) Color: #8241*

7 (7, 8, 8) balls Gedifra Tecno Hair *100yds (90m) 50g (100% nylon) Color: #9609*

NEEDLES

US #10.5 (6.5mm) 16" (40.5cm) circular and single pointed long needles, and US #10 (6 mm) short single pointed or size needed to obtain gauge.

GAUGE

In Stockinette Stitch pattern 12 sts and 15 rows = 4" (10cm).

FINISHED SIZES

Chest 36 (38, 40, 42)" / 91 (96.5, 101.5, 106.5)cm.

Length 24.75 (25, 25.5, 26)" / 63 (64, 65, 66)cm.

Sleeve length 18 (18, 18, 18.5)" / 45.5 (45.5, 45.5, 47)cm.

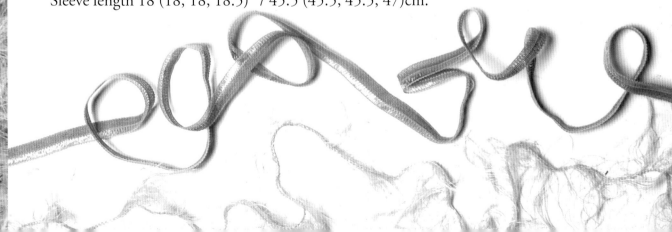

CUDDLY PULLOVER

BACK

With 1 strand of each yarn held tog, cast on 53 (56, 59, 62) sts. Work in St st for 6" (15cm). (RS) Dec 1 st at each end of next and foll 8th row = 49 (52, 55, 58) sts. Work 7 rows even St st. Inc 1 st at each end of next and foll 8th row = 53 (56, 59, 62) sts. Cont even St st until back measures 16 (16.5, 16.5, 17)" / 40.5 (42, 42, 43).

SHAPE ARMHOLES

Bind off 3 sts at beg of next 2 rows. Dec 1 st at each end of next 2 (3,4,5) rows = 43 (44, 45, 46) sts ** Work even St st until armhole measures 8.75 (8.75, 9, 9)" / 22 (22, 23, 23)cm. Bind off.

FRONT

Work as for back up to **. Work even St st until armhole measures 6" (15cm).

SHAPE NECK

(RS) K17, turn, leave rem sts on holder. (WS) Purl.

Work 4 rows dec 1 st at neck edge in every row = 13 sts.

Work even St st until armhole measures same as back. Bind off.

With RS facing slip 9 (10, 11, 12) sts onto holder, join yarn to rem 17 sts and K to end. Complete to match first side of neck reversing shaping.

SLEEVES (make two)

Work 9 rows even. Inc 1 st at each end of next and every foll 4th row, three times 38 (39, 40, 41) sts, then every foll 6th row four times = 46 (47, 48, 49) sts. Work even until sleeve measures 17 (16.5, 16.5, 16.5)" / 43

(42, 42, 42)cm. Bind off 3 sts loosely at beg of next 2 rows = 40 (41, 42, 43) sts. Work 2 (3, 4, 5) rows dec 1 st each end of every row = 36 (35, 34, 33) sts. Bind off.

FINISHING

Crochet shoulder seams (p.21). With 16" circular needles and right side of work facing, pick up and knit (p.22)17 (18, 19, 20) sts at back of neck, 11 sts along left side of neck, K 9 (10, 11, 12) sts from stitch

holder, pick up and knit (p.22) 11sts along right side of neck = 48 (50, 52, 54) sts. Purl in the round for 7" (18cm). RS tog crochet sleeve caps centered to shoulder and finish sleeves and side seams.

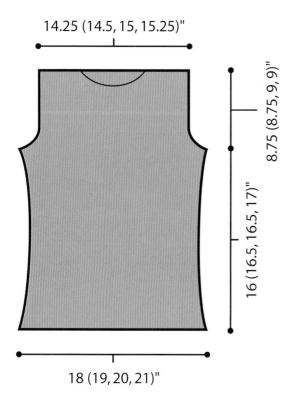

14.25 (14.5, 15, 15.25)"

8.75 (8.75, 9, 9)"

16 (16.5, 16.5, 17)"

18 (19, 20, 21)"

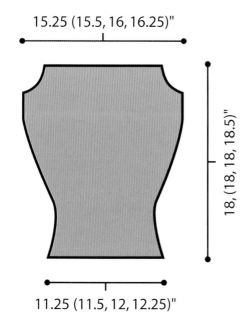

15.25 (15.5, 16, 16.25)"

18, (18, 18, 18.5)"

11.25 (11.5, 12, 12.25)"

CUDDLY PULLOVER SCARF

With US #10 short single pointed and 1 strand of each yarn held tog cast on 28 sts. Work Garter st for 6" (15cm). Drop Tecno Hair and continue in Zen alone. Inc row: K2 (M1, K6) 4 times, K2 = 32 sts. Work in a double moss st until scarf measures 60" (152cm).

Rows 1 & 2: (K1, P1) rep.

Rows 3 & 4: (P1, K1) rep.

Add Tecno Hair and work both strands held tog. Dec row: K2 (K2tog, K5) 4 times, K2 = 28 sts. Work in Garter st for only 3" (7.5cm). Bind off loosely.

TECHNIQUES

Counting Rows When Shaping (p.14)

Picking Up Stitches Around the Neck (p.22)

Long Chenille Vest

A must-have vest that can be dressed up or down and always looks sharp. This pattern knits up beautifully holding two different yarns together throughout. The design features easy, built-in Garter stitch borders and collar for minimal seaming. The firm chenille texture allows the collar to stand up. This versatile vest will become a favorite.

YARN

6 (7, 8, 9) hanks Crystal Palace Cotton Chenille *98yds (88m) 50g (100% cotton) Color: #9598*

2 (2, 3, 3) balls Plymouth Eros *165yds (148m) 50g (100% nylon) Color: #1024*

2 (2, 3, 3) balls Plymouth 24K *187yds (168m) 50g (82% nylon, 18% lamé) Color: #1372*

2 (2, 3, 3) balls Plymouth Electra *125yds (112m) 50g (100% nylon) Color: #48*

NEEDLES

US #7 (4.50mm) long single pointed needles and US #6 (4.00mm) or size needed to obtain gauge.

GAUGE

In Stockinette Stitch pattern 15 sts and 24 rows = 4" (10cm) using US #7 needles and alternating yarns following the color sequence.

FINISHED SIZES

Chest 40 (44, 48, 52)" / 101.5 (112, 122, 132)cm.

Length 26 (27.5, 29, 30.5)" / 66 (70, 73.5, 77.5)cm.

COLOR SEQUENCE

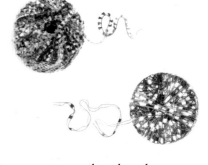

A: Main color + Eros held tog work 2 rows

B: Main color + 24K held tog work 2 rows

C: Main color + Electra held tog work 2 rows

Repeat colors A - C working 2 rows of each always twisting yarns at each color change thereby carrying up the colors along the side of the work instead of cutting them each time.

LONG CHENILLE VEST

BACK

With US #7 needles and color A cast on 75 (82, 90, 98) sts. Knit 4 rows.

*Row 1: (RS) Knit.

Row 2: (WS) K4, P to last 4 sts, K4.

* Rep last two rows until work measures 5" (13cm). Slits are done. Continue in St st until work measures 17 (18, 19, 20)" / 43 (45.5, 48, 51)cm. Next row: (RS) Knit.

Next row: (WS) K10, P to last 10 sts, K10. Repeat last two rows 2 more times.

ARMHOLE SHAPING

Next row: (RS) Knit.

Next row: (WS) K10, P to last 10 sts, K10.

Repeat last two rows 2 more times.

Next row: (RS) Bind off 6 sts, K to end.

Next row: (WS) Bind off 6 sts, K3, P to last 4 sts, K4.

Repeat rows 1 and 2 from * to * until armhole measures 8 (8.5, 9, 9.5)" / 20.5 (21.5, 23, 24)cm. Place rem 63 (70, 78, 86) sts on a holder.

LEFT FRONT

With US #7 needles and color A cast on 42 (45, 49, 52) sts.

Knit 4 rows.

Row 1: (RS) Knit.

Row 2: (WS) K4, P to last 4 sts, K4. Rep last two rows until work measures 5" (13cm). Slits are done.

Next row: (RS) Knit.

Next row: (WS) K4, P to end.

Continue repeating last two rows until work measures 17 (18, 19, 20)" / 43 (45.5, 48, 51)cm.

Next row: (RS) Knit.

Next row: (WS) K4, P to last 10 sts, K10. Repeat last two rows twice.

ARMHOLE SHAPING

Next row: (RS) Bind off 6 sts, K to end.

Next row: (WS) K16, P to last 4 sts, K4.

Next row: (RS) Knit.

Repeat last two rows until armhole measures 8 (8.5, 9, 9.5)" / 20.5 (21.5, 23, 24)cm. ending on a WS row. RS facing transfer sts from Back onto separate needle ready for WS row, and join 20 (23, 27, 30) shoulder sts RS tog working 3-needle bind off (p.20). Place rem sts on a holder: 16 front sts and 43 (47, 51, 56) sts from back.

RIGHT FRONT

With US #7 needles and color A cast on 42 (45, 49, 52) sts.

Knit 4 rows.

Row 1: (RS) Knit.

Row 2: (WS) K4, P to last 4 sts, K4.

Rep last two rows until work measures 5" (13cm).

Next row: (RS) Knit.

Next row: (WS) P to last 4 sts, K4.

Continue repeating last two rows until work measures 17 (18, 19, 20)" / 43 (45.5, 48, 51)cm.

Next row: (RS) Knit.

Next row: (WS) K10, P to last 4 sts, K4. Repeat last two rows twice.

Next row: (RS) Knit.

ARMHOLE SHAPING

Next row: (WS) Bind off 6 sts, K4, P to last 4 sts, K4.

Next row: (RS) Knit.

Next row: (WS) K4, P to last 16 sts, K16.

Repeat last two rows until armhole measures 8 (8.5, 9, 9.5)" / 20.5 (21.5, 23, 24)cm. ending on a RS row. WS facing transfer sts from Back onto separate needle ready for RS row, and join 20 (23, 27, 30) shoulder sts RS tog working 3-needle bind off (p.20).

COLLAR

Slip remaining sts back onto needle, join yarn RS facing, and K across front sts, pick up and knit (p.22) 1 st before and after

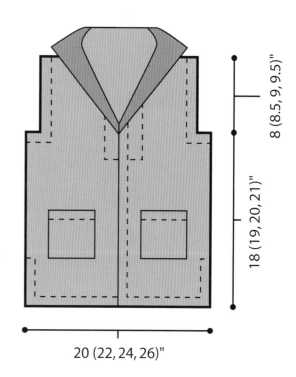

8 (8.5, 9, 9.5)"

18 (19, 20, 21)"

20 (22, 24, 26)"

shoulder seam, K across back sts, pick up and knit 1 st before and after shoulder seam, K across front sts = 79 (83, 87, 92) sts. Work in Garter stitch rows until collar measures 4" (10cm) from shoulder. Bind off.

POCKETS (make two)
With US #6 needles and Cotton Chenille cast on 20 sts. Work in St stitch rows for 4" (10cm). Knit 6 rows of Garter stitch. Bind off.

FINISHING

Center pockets on right and left front above side slits, pin, and sew into place. RS together crochet side seams (p.21). Weave in all ends.

TECHNIQUES

3-Needle Bind Off (p.20)

Crochet Seams (p.21)

Picking Up Stitches (p.22)

Blocking (p.24)

Backdrop Pullover

Knit a great sweater using a variety of yarns in a simple Stockinette stitch drop shoulder pattern. Work alternating novelty yarns carried together with the same basic yarn throughout. The more textures and colors the better against the solid color backdrop yarn. The base yarn supports even the most slippery novelty yarns and will keep them together as you knit. V-neck shawl collar is worked separately in your favorite yarn combination.

YARN

MC: 5 (6, 7) balls Rowan Kid Classic *151yds (140m) 50g (70% lambs wool, 26% kid mohair, 4% nylon) Color: #841*

A: 2 (3, 3) balls Needful San José *60yds (55m) 50g (82% nylon, 18% viscose) Color: #4186*

B: 1 (1, 2) hanks Colinette Giotto *160yds (148m) 100g (50% cotton, 40% rayon, 10% nylon) Color: Gauguin*

C: 1 (1, 2) balls Ironstone Paris Nights *202yds (186m) 50g (67% acrylic, 21% nylon, 12% metal) Color: #22*

D: 1 (2, 2) balls Lana Gatto Andalusia *120yds (110m) 50g (100% nylon) Color: #4000*

E: 2 (3, 3) balls Ironstone Desert Flower *126yds (116m) 50g (88% viscose, 7% polyester, 5% metalized thread) Color: #18*

NEEDLES

US #10.5 (6.5mm) and US #11 (8mm) long single pointed or size needed to obtain gauge.

GAUGE

In Stockinette Stitch pattern 12 sts and 16 rows = 4" (10cm) using US #11 needles and alternating yarns following the color sequence.

FINISHED SIZES

Chest 39 (43, 47)" / 99 (109, 119)cm.

Length 21.5 (23, 24.5)" / 55 (58, 62)cm.

Sleeve Length 16.5" (42cm).

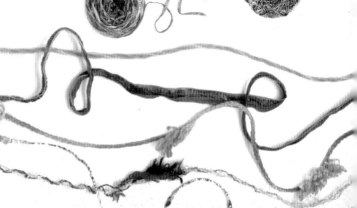

Dressy Yoke Top and Cape

This ensemble features a dressy yoke top and matching cape. The timeless chic top is knit in soft suede and crisp ribbon yarns held together. It's worked in the round on circular needles with minimal finishing. The lightweight, soft cape is knit in Garter stitch on big needles with nylon, kid mohair, and wool yarns. The body is worked loosely on big needles with shaped shoulders and has a shimmering ribbon border. Simply stunning!

YARN

Dressy Yoke Top

2 (2, 3, 3) balls Plymouth Eros Glitz *158yds (145m) 50g (86% nylon, 10% rayon, 4% lurex) Color: #117*

4 (4, 5, 6) balls Berroco Suede *120yds (111m) 50g (100% nylon) Color: #3729*

6 (7, 8, 9) balls Berroco Zen *110yds (102m) 50g (55% cotton 45% nylon) Color: #8253*

1 (1, 1, 1.25) yds elastic band 3/8" wide

Cape

1 ball Plymouth Eros Glitz *158yds (142m) 50g (86% nylon, 10% rayon, 4% lurex) Color: #117*

1 ball Berroco Suede *120yds (111m) 50g (100% nylon) Color: #3729*

2 balls Plymouth Flirt *93yds (83m) 50g (100% nylon) Color: #16*

2 balls Plassard Flore *98yds (90m) 50g (75% kid mohair, 20% wool, 5% polyamide) Color: #15*

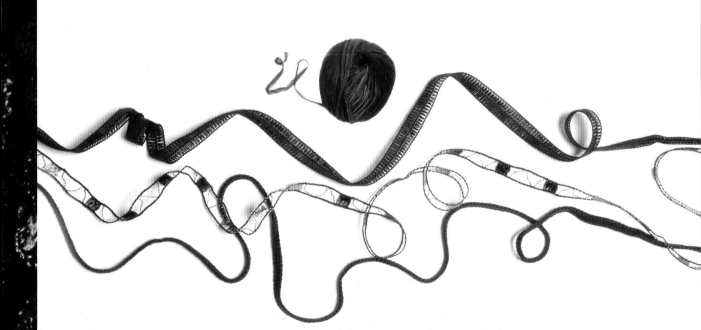

NEEDLES

Dressy Yoke Top

US #9 (5.5mm) and US #10.5 (6.5mm) 29" (73.5cm) circular and double pointed needles in both sizes or size needed to obtain gauge.

Cape

US #15 (10mm) long single pointed or 24" (61cm) circular, and US #17 (12.75mm) long single pointed or 24" circular needles.

GAUGE

Dressy Yoke Top

In Stockinette Stitch 14 sts and 20 rows = 4" (10cm) using US #10.5 needles and 1 strand of Suede and Zen held tog.

Cape

In Garter Stitch pattern 8 sts and 14 rows = 4" (10cm) using US #17 needles and 1 strand Flirt and Flore held tog.

FINISHED SIZES

Dressy Yoke Top

Chest 34 (38, 42, 46)" / 86 (96.5, 106.5, 117)cm.

Length 19.5 (20.5, 22, 23)" / 50 (52, 56, 58.5)cm.

Cape

One size fits all.

DRESSY YOKE TOP

BODY

With US #9 29" circular needles and 1 strand of Zen and Eros Glitz held tog, cast on 120 (134, 148, 162) sts. Place a stitch marker (p.13) and join in the round (p.12) working four rounds of Garter st as follows:

Rnd 1: Knit.

Rnd 2: Purl. Repeat last two rnds.

Change to US #10.5 29" circular needles and 1 strand of Zen and Suede held tog. Knit in the round in St st until piece measures 10 (10.5, 11, 11.5)" / 25.5 (26.5, 28, 29)cm. Change to US #9 29" circular needles and 1 strand of Zen and Eros Glitz held tog and purl 10 (12, 14, 16) rnds. Bind off 3 (3, 4, 4) sts, P54 (61, 66,

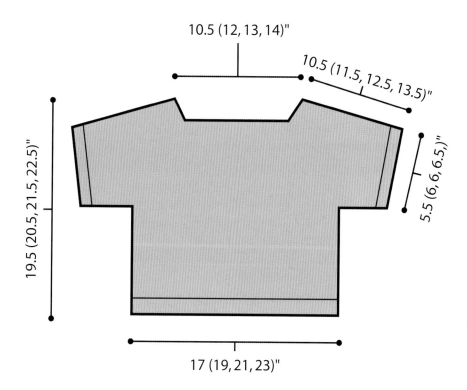

10.5 (12, 13, 14)"

10.5 (11.5, 12.5, 13.5)"

19.5 (20.5, 21.5, 22.5)"

5.5 (6, 6, 6.5)"

17 (19, 21, 23)"

73) sts, bind off 6 (6, 8, 8) sts, P54 (61, 66, 73) sts, bind off 3 (3, 4, 4) sts. Hold work aside.

SLEEVES

With US #9 double pointed needles and 1 strand of Zen and Eros held tog, cast on 36 (40, 43, 46) sts. Place marker (p.13) and join in the round (p.12) working four rnds of Garter stitch as follows:

Round 1: Knit.

Round 2: Purl. Repeat last two rounds.

Change to #10.5 double pointed needles and 1 strand of Zen and Suede held tog. Knit in St st increasing 1 st at beg and end of every 4th rnd 3 times (p.14) until 42 (46, 49, 52) sts. Work even 1 (2, 3, 4) rnds. Change to US #9 double pointed needles and 1 strand of Zen and Eros Glitz held tog and purl 10 (12, 14, 16) rnds.

SHAPE CAP OF SLEEVE

(RS) Bind off 3 (3, 4, 4) sts, P36 (40, 41, 44), bind off 3 (3, 4, 4) sts. Leave on holder. Make another sleeve to match.

TECHNIQUES

Dressy Yoke Top

Joining in the Round (p.12)

Working with Stitch Markers (p.13)

Counting Rows when Shaping (p.14)

Yarn Over (p.15)

Crochet Seams (p.21)

Blocking (p.24)

Openwork Pullover and Sheer Scarf

You'll be a hit with this chic style pullover featuring knit lace inserts and puffed sleeves. The top is knit in a cool linen yarn in Stockinette stitch, and off set with a multi-colored sheer ribbon in small patterned sections. Clear instructions teach you how to shape within a stitch pattern and bridge gauges when changing stitch patterns. Matching two-sided scarf is worked in a simple one-row pattern.

YARN

11 (11, 12) balls Maggi Knits Maggi's Linen *126yds (116m) 50g (52% cotton, 48% linen) Color: #07*

2 balls Gerifil Binarone *166yds (153m) 50g (100% nylon) Color: #151*

FINISHED SIZES

38 (42, 46)" / 96.5 (107, 117)cm.

NEEDLES

US #9 (5.5mm), US #10 (6mm), US #19 (15mm) long single pointed needles, and US #7 (5mm) 16" (41cm) circular needles or size needed to obtain gauge.

GAUGE

Body: In Stockinette Stitch pattern 14 sts and 20 rows = 4" (10cm) with US#10 needles and 2 strands of Maggi's Linen held tog. Sleeves: In Stockinette Stitch pattern 16 sts and 20 rows = 4" (10cm) with US#9 needles and 1 strand of Maggi's Linen.

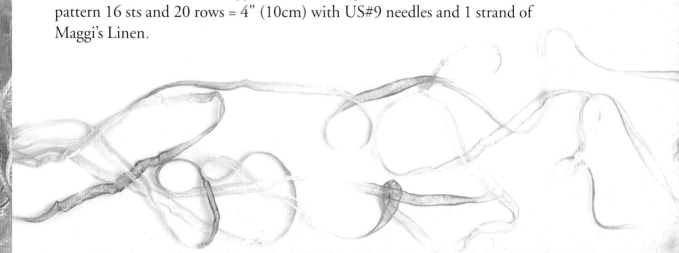

OPENWORK PULLOVER

BACK

LACE BORDER

With US #9 needles and 1 strand of Binarone cast on 101 (111, 121) sts and work lace border as follows:

Row 1: (RS) Knit.

Row 2: (WS) P1, * yrn (p.15), P3, [sl (p.18) next 2 sts tog purlwise, P1, pass the 2 slipped sts over], P3, yrn, P1, rep from * to end.

Row 3: (RS) K1, * K1, yfwd (p.15), K2, [sl next 2 sts tog knitwise, K1, pass the 2 slipped sts over], K2, yfwd, K2, rep from * to end.

Row 4: (WS) P1, * P2, yrn, P1, [sl next 2 sts tog purlwise, P1, pass the 2 slipped sts over], P1, yrn, P3, rep from * to end.

Row 5: (RS) K1, * K3, yfwd, [sl next 2 sts tog knitwise, K1, pass the 2 slipped sts over], yfwd, K4, rep from * to end.

Row 6: (WS) P1, * P1, K2, P2, rep from * to end.

Row 7: (RS) K1, * yfwd, sl 1, K1, psso, P1, yo (p.15), [sl next 2 sts tog knitwise, K1, pass the 2 slipped sts over], yrn, P1, K2tog, yfwd, K1, rep from * to end.

Row 8: (WS) P1, * P2, K1, P3, K1, P3, rep from * to end.

Row 9: (RS) K1, * K1, yfwd, sl 1, K1, psso, yfwd, [sl next 2 sts tog knitwise, K1, pass the 2 slipped sts over], yfwd, K2tog, yfwd, K2, rep from * to end.

Row 10: (WS) P1, * P1, K1, P5, K1, P2, rep from * to end.

Row 11: (RS) K1, * K1, P1, K1, yfwd, [sl next 2 sts tog knitwise, K1, pass the 2 slipped sts

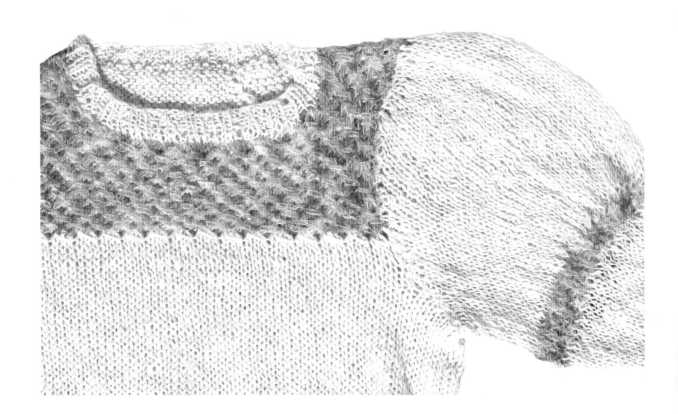

over], yfwd, K1, P1, K2, rep from * to end.

Row 12: (WS) Rep row 10.

Rows 13–16: Knit.

Change to US #10 needles and 2 strands Maggi's Linen held tog (p.18) and work dec row to bridge the different gauges (p.17).

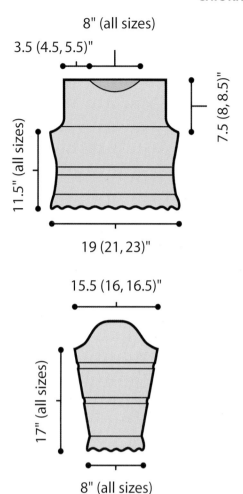

Size S: K2tog (K1, K2tog) rep to end = 68 sts.

Size M: (K1, K2tog) = 74 sts.

Size L: (K1, K2tog) rep to last st, K1 = 81 sts.

SHAPE BODY (p.14)

Work 4 rows St st. *Dec row: SSK, K to last 2 sts, K2tog. Work 3 rows St st.* Rep from * to *. Dec row: SSK, K to last 2 sts, K2tog = 62 (68, 75) sts. P1 row.

Change to US #9 needles and 1 strand Binarone (p.18) and work 6 rows (K1, P1) ribbing. Change to US #10 needles and 2 strands Maggi's Linen held tog (p.18)

** Inc row: K1, M1, K to last st, M1, K1. Work 3 rows St st. ** Rep from ** to **.

Inc row: K1, M1, K to last st, M1, K1 = 68 (74, 81) sts. Work St st until work measures 11.5" (29cm), or desired length.

SHAPE ARMHOLE

Bind off 5 sts at the beg of next two rows. Bind off 1 st at the beg of next four rows = 54 (60, 67) sts rem. Work even until work measures 19 (19.5, 20)" / 48 (49.5, 51)cm. Bind off.

FRONT

Work as for back to shape armhole. WS facing, bind off 5 sts at the beg of next two rows. Bind off 1 st at the beg of next four rows = 54 (60, 67) sts rem.

LACE YOKE

WS facing change to 1 strand Binarone (p.18) and inc 12 (12, 11) sts evenly (p.17) = 66 (72, 78) sts.

Row 1: (RS) K2, *yo (p.15), sl 1 (p.18), K2, pass slip st over both K sts*, rep from * to *, ending K1.

Row 2: (WS) Purl.

Row 3: (RS) K1, *sl 1, K2, pass slip st over both K sts, yo *, rep from * to *, ending K2.

Row 4: (WS) Purl. Rep patt 4 more times, then rep rows 1-3 once ending RS row.

SHAPE NECK

WS facing purl 21 (24, 27) sts, bind off 24 sts, purl rem 21 (24, 27) sts.

LEFT SHOULDER

Dec row 1: (RS) K2, *yo, sl 1, K2, pass slip st over both K sts *, rep from * to * until 4 sts rem, yo, sl 1, K2tog, psso, K1.

Dec row 2: (WS) P2tog, purl to end.

Dec row 3: (RS) K1, *sl 1, K2, pass slip st over both K sts, yo *, rep from * to * until 3 sts rem, K1, K2tog. Purl 1 row. Cont in lace pattern on rem 18 (21, 24) sts until front measures 19 (19.5, 20)" / 48 (49.5, 51)cm. Bind off.

RIGHT SHOULDER

Dec row 1: (RS) K2tog, *yo, sl 1, K2, pass slip st over both K sts *, rep from * to *, ending K1.
Dec row 2: (WS) Purl to last 2 sts, P2tog.
Dec row 3: (RS) K2tog, *sl 1, K2, pass slip st over both K sts, yo *, rep from * to *, ending K2. Purl 1 row.

Continue in lace patt on rem 18 (21, 24) sts until front measures 19 (19.5, 20)" / 48 (49.5, 51)cm. Bind off.

SLEEVES

With US #9 needles and 1 strand of Binarone cast on 41 sts and work 16 rows of lace border. Change to 1 strand Maggi's Linen (p.18) and dec 9 (7, 5) sts evenly (p.17) = 32 (34, 36) sts. Working in St st inc 1 st at beg and end of every 3rd row 7 times (p.14) = 46 (48, 50) sts. Change to 1 strand Binarone (p.18) and work 6 rows (K1, P1) ribbing. Change to 1 strand Maggi's Linen (p.18) and cont St st inc 1 st at beg and end of every 3rd row 8 times (p.14) = 62 (64, 66) sts. Work even St st until sleeve measures 13" (33 cm). Change to 1 strand Binarone (p.18) and work 6 rows (K1, P1) ribbing. Change to 1 strand Maggi's Linen (p.18) and cont St

st beg with one inc row for the puffed sleeve: K19 (20, 21) sts, Inc 1 in each of the next 24 sts, K19 (20, 21) sts = 86 (88, 90) st. Work even until sleeve measures 17" (43 cm).

SHAPE CAP

Bind off 6 sts at the beg of next two rows. Bind off 1 st at the beg of next four rows = 70 (72, 74) sts. Cont shaping cap by binding off 1 st at the beg of every row until 50 sts. Dec row for the puffed sleeve: (RS) K2tog in every st = 25 sts. Bind off.

FINISHING

RS tog crochet shoulder seams tog (p.21). With US #7 16" (41 cm) circular needles, and 1 strand of Maggi's Linen pick up and knit (p.22) 28 sts across back, 25 sts along left front, and 25 sts along right front = 78 sts. Work in K2, P2 ribbing for 5 rnds. Bind off loosely. RS tog crochet sleeve caps centered to shoulder and finish sleeves and side seams. Block finished sweater.

SHEER SCARF

With US #19 needles and 1 strand of Binarone cast on 22 sts. Patt row: * K1, yfwd (p.15), slip 1 purlwise (p.18), rep from * to end of row. Rep patt row until 54" (137 cm) or desired length. Bind off.

TECHNIQUES

Counting Rows when Shaping (p.14)

Yarn Over (p.15)

Bridging Different Gauges (p.17)

Vintage Purse

A great comeback for the little evening purse is this vintage inspired knitted pouch with silver frame. A simple slip stitch pattern in alternating ribbon yarns adds style and texture. Easy-to-mount frame is sewn on through indented framework. Great accessory for any festive occasion.

YARN

1 hank Plymouth Eros Extreme *98yds (88m) 100g (100% nylon) Color: #314*

2 balls Plymouth Odyssey Glitz *65yds (58m) 50g (60% nylon, 37% wool, 3% lamé) Color: #919*

MATERIALS

3 ft (2.75m) Lacis Purse Frame Chain #LS71 Color: Silver

1 Lacis Purse Frame #LS78 Color: Silver

NEEDLES

US #10 (6mm) 24" (61cm) circular needles or size needed to obtain gauge.

GAUGE

In Garter Stitch pattern 17 sts and 28 rows = 4" (10cm) using US #10 needles and 1 strand of Eros Extreme.

SIZE

7" (18cm) wide x 8" (20.5cm) tall.

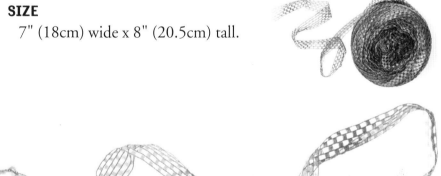

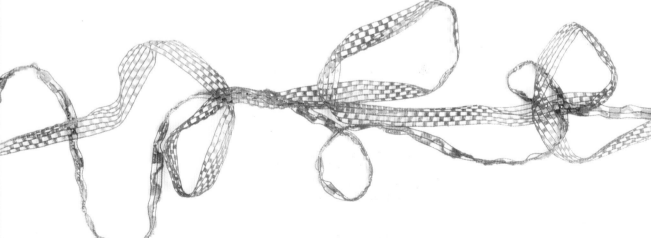

VINTAGE PURSE

BOTTOM

Cast on 32 sts using US #10 needles and 1 strand Eros Extreme. Knit 18 rows in Garter stitch. Bottom of bag is complete. Now pick up sts around bottom to knit bag in the round as follows: Place marker (p.13), pick up and knit (p.22) 8 sts along short end, place marker, pick up and knit 32 sts, place marker, pick up and knit 8 sts, place different color marker for end of round = 80 sts. Join to work in rnds.

*Round 1: Using Odyssey Glitz (P1, yfwd, slip 4 sts purlwise) rep around.

Note: Stretch the sts on the RH needle between every purl st.

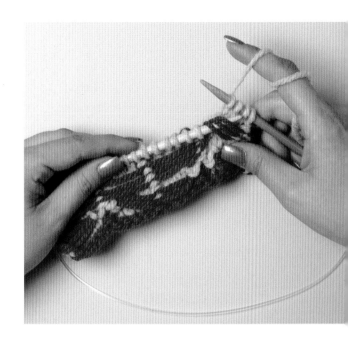

Round 2: Using Eros Extreme, K1 rnd. Repeat rnds 1 and 2 two more times.

FLOATS ROUND

Using Eros Extreme (P1, K3, take up floats by inserting LH needle under the three slipped threads and P tog with next stitch, P1, take up floats by inserting LH needle

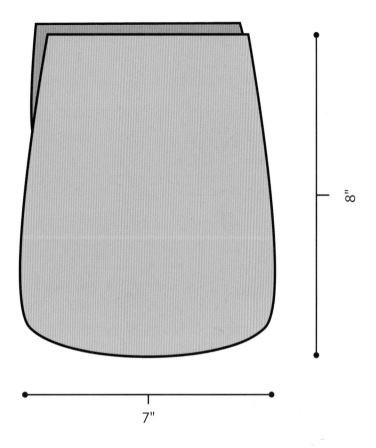

8"

7"

under the three slipped threads and P tog with next stitch, K3) rep around.* Repeat from *to* five more times.

SEPARATE FOR PURSE FRAME

Turn * Row 1: (WS) Using Eros Extreme P2tog, P to last 2 sts, P2tog.

Row 2: (RS) Using Eros Extreme K2tog, K to last 2 sts, K2tog. Change to Odyssey Glitz and rep row 1 and 2 two times.

Last row: (WS) (P1, P2tog) rep across.

Bind off. Join yarn on other side wrong side facing and repeat from *.

FINISHING

Using small sewing needle and sewing thread attach purse frame by stitching through the small holes around the frame starting on one side and easing in the width of the bag as you stitch across.

Repeat on other side of frame. Join chain to purse frame loops using nose head pliers.

TECHNIQUES

Slipped Stitches (p.18)

Picking Up Stitches (p.22)

Taking Up Floats

Felted Messenger Tote

A roomy companion bag with a sense of flair to hold both your knitting projects and books. Knits up quickly in the round with two strands of wool held together. Sturdy strap is knit onto bag and felted together. Knit the fur flap in simple Garter stitch rows decreased to a point over the center of the bag. A carry-all tote for every occasion.

YARN AND MATERIALS

2 hanks Ironstone New Wool *292yds (270m) (95% wool, 5% polyester) Color: #5012*

2 skeins Brown Sheep Lamb's Pride Worsted *190yds (175m) (85% wool, 15% mohair) Color: #M-89 Roasted Coffee*

1 ball Plymouth Furlauro *82yds (75m) 50g (100% nylon) Color: #830*

2 yds colorfast waste cotton in a worsted weight, 4" (10cm) gros grain ribbon and one magnetic snap.

NEEDLES

US #10 (6mm) long single pointed, US #10.5 (6.5mm) short single pointed, and US #11 (8mm) 29" (73.5cm) circular needles or size needed to obtain gauge.

GAUGE

In Stockinette Stitch pattern using US #11 needles before felting, 11 sts and 14 rows = 4" (10cm) and 1 strand of Lamb's Pride Worsted and New Wool held tog.

FINISHED SIZE

After felting approx 14" (35.5cm) wide x 10" (25cm) tall x 4" (10cm) deep.

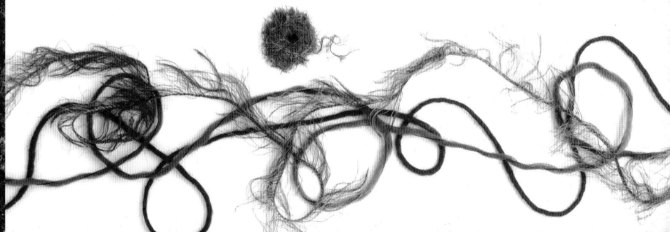

FELTED MESSENGER TOTE

BAG

With US #11 circular needles and 1 strand of Lamb's Pride Worsted and New Wool held tog, cast on 48 sts. Knit in Garter st 30 rows. Bottom of bag is done. Now pick up sts around bottom to knit bag in the round as follows: place a marker (p.13) on RH needle, pick up and knit (p.22)16 sts along short end of fabric to next corner, place another marker on RH needle, pick up and knit 48 sts to next corner, place another marker on RH needle, pick up and knit 16 sts to next corner, place a different color marker to indicate beginning of round = 128 sts. Join to work in rnds. Knit 1 rnd. Next rnd: Slip 1 (p.18) (K to marker, pm, slip 1) rep around. Repeat last two rnds 25 more times = 52 total rnds completed.

Work in Garter stitch as follows:

Round 1: Purl.

Round 2: Knit.

Repeat last two rnds three more times = 60 total rnds completed. Next rnd bind off and set up stitches for strap and flap as follows: K4 (K2tog, K2) 10 times, K4 to first marker, bind off 2 sts, K 12 sts and place on holder, bind off 52 sts, knit 12 sts and place on holder, bind off 2 sts. Change to US #10 needles and waste cotton and K38 sts. Turn. Bind off 38 sts.

STRAP

With US #10.5 (6.5mm) needles and 1 strand of Lamb's Pride Worsted cast on 12 sts. Knit in Garter st until strap measures 40". *Transfer 12 sts from holder onto US #10.5 needles WS facing. Join straps

(Measurements before felting)

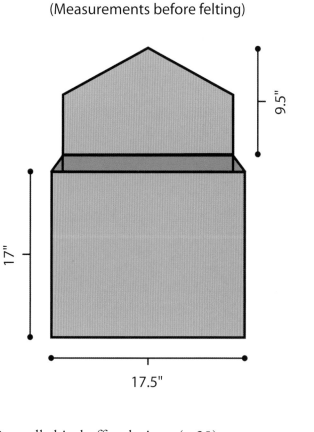

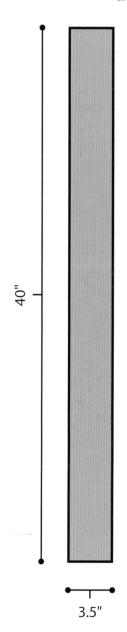

using the 3-needle bind off technique (p.20). Repeat from * on opposite side of bag. Felt Bag (p.19)

FUR FLAP

Pick up and knit (p.22) 38 sts on the felted bag using US #10 needles and 1 strand New Wool. Add Furlauro and knit in Garter st for 30 rows holding two strands tog. Shape flap as follows: K1, SSK, K to last 3 sts, K2tog, K1. Repeat last row until 2 sts remain. Bind off.

FINISHING

Comb the fur yarns to make flap furrier. Attach magnetic snap to a piece of gros grain ribbon and sew to inside of flap.

TECHNIQUES

Working with Stitch Markers (p.13)

Slipped Stitches (p.18)

Felting (p.19)

Bridging Felt with Knitting (p.19)

3-Needle Bind Off (p.20)

Picking Up Stitches (p.22)

Felted Chenille Bag

This felted chenille bag will become a favorite with faded aran stitches in a soft crushed velvet. The roomy bag is lined and mounted with ready-made suede handles. Embellished with bead tassels, this charming bag is an ideal travel companion that will carry your knitting projects in style.

YARN

6 balls Muench Touch Me *61yds (55m) 50g (72% rayon micro fibers, 28% new wool) Color: #3623*

MATERIALS

1 Yarn Craft Suede Sew on Handles

2 Renaissance Buttons SI16463/42TAU

2 Expo Intl bead tassel SM3654GY

NEEDLES

US #8 (5mm) 29" (73.5cm) circular and double pointed needles or size needed to obtain gauge.

GAUGE

In Stockinette Stitch pattern before felting, 13 sts and 19 rows = 4" (10cm).

FINISHED SIZE

After felting approx 16" (41cm) wide x 11" (28cm) tall x 4.5" (12cm) deep.

ABBREVIATIONS

T2, 3-st right cross, 3-st left cross, C4B, C4F, C6B, C6F, Make bobble (p.24).

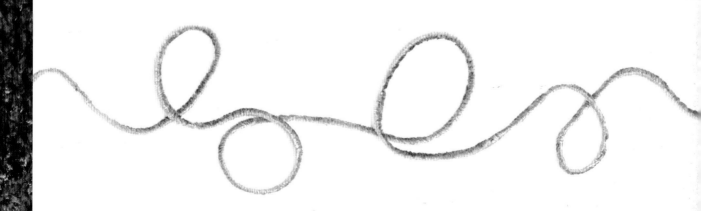

Felted Jazz Bag

Jazz up your basic felt bag with a knitted band embellished with coordinating beads and strands of novelty yarns. Felt the strap and join to bag with a 3-needle bind off. Learn how to complete a self-made button, beaded tassel, and loop closure using the same yarns. Great accessory for all occasions.

YARN

1 ball Brown Sheep Lamb's Pride Worsted *190yds (173m) 113g (85% wool 15% mohair) Color: #M-77 Blue Magic*

1 hank Manos del Uruguay Wool *138yds (126m) 100g (100% wool) Color: #61*

Embellishment Village Bead & Yarn Kit #19000-PUR-B

1 spool knitting wire 28 gauge (40 yds) Color: Silver (10yds) (9m)

1 strand colorfast waste cotton in a dk weight

NEEDLES

US #8 (5mm) and US #10.5 (6.5mm) 29" (73.5cm) circular needles or size needed to obtain gauge.

Crochet hook size F.

GAUGE

Unfelted, in Stockinette Stitch pattern 14 sts and 18 rows = 4" (10cm) using US #10.5 needles and 1 strand of Lamb's Pride Worsted.

FINISHED SIZE

After felting, 10" (25cm) x 10" (25cm).

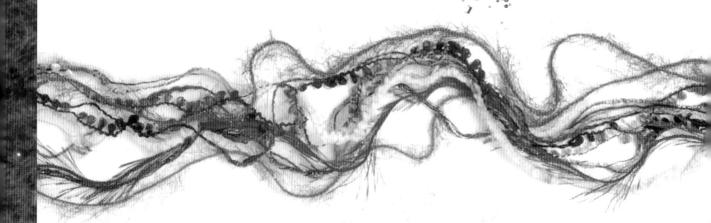

FELTED JAZZ BAG

BASE

Using 1 strand of Lamb's Pride Worsted and 10.5 circular needles, cast on 40 sts. Work 40 rows in Garter st. Bottom of bag is done. Now pick up sts around bottom to knit bag in the rnd as follows: Next row (RS) Place a marker (p.13) on the needle, pick up and knit (p.22)19 sts along short end, place marker, pick up 40 sts along long end, place marker, pick up 19 sts along other short end, place a different color marker for beg of rnd = 118 sts. Join to work in rnds.

Knit 1 rnd. Next rnd *K to marker, pm, slip 1 (p.18), K to last st before marker, slip 1, pm*, rep from *. Repeat last two rnds two more times = 6 rnds completed. Change to Manos and continue rep last two rnds for another 40 rnds. Change to US #8 needles and waste cotton in dk weight and work one dec rnd. As follows: K2tog *K4, K2tog*, rep from *, end K2tog = 97 sts. Knit one more rnd. Bind off. Felt Bag Using Washing Machine (p.19).

BAND

Pick up 96 sts using the Joining Felt with Knitting technique (p.19). As follows with right side facing, start at the side gusset, pick up sts at the base of the first row of waste cotton by drawing loops through, using a crochet hook and then transferring sts onto US #8 circular needle. Cut bind off corner of waste cotton and unravel all the cotton. Place marker and knit one round. Open embellishment kit and tie novelty strands together with overhand knots into stash yarn. String beads onto knitting wire, saving largest beads for button closure.

BEADS

Slide beads (a group of beads approx 1/4") in front, slip 1, move wire to back, grab bead cluster in front, and twist the wire to keep beads in front.

BEGIN PATTERN

Rnd 1: Using stash yarn from the kit, *K1, yfwd, slip 3* (p.18), rep from * to * to end of rnd.

Rnd 2: Using Lamb's Pride K2 ***Beads,** K3 using Lamb's Pride*, rep from * to *, end **Beads**, K1.

Rnd 3: Using stash yarn yfwd slip 2 *K1, yfwd slip 3*, rep from * to *, end K1, yfwd slip 1.

Rnd 4: ***Beads**, K3 using Lamb's Pride*, rep from * to *.

Rnd 5: Using Novelty yarn from the kit, *K1, slip 3*, rep from * to *.

Rnd 6: Knit using Lamb's Pride.

Rnd 7: Purl using Lamb's Pride.

Rnd 8: K6, bind off 36, K12, bind off 36, K6. Leave on needle.

MAKE STRAP

Using US #10.5 needle and Lamb's Pride Worsted, cast on 12 sts. Knit 40 rows always slipping first st of every row. Dec row: Slip 1, K2tog, K to last 2 sts, K2tog = 10 sts. Knit 20 rows always slipping first st of every row. Dec row: Slip 1, K2tog, K to last 2 sts, K2tog = 8 sts. Knit 80 rows always slipping first st of every row. Inc row: Slip 1, Inc 1, K to last st, Inc 1 = 10 sts. Knit 20 rows always slipping first st of every row. Inc row: Slip 1, Inc 1, K to last st, Inc 1 = 12 sts. Knit 40 rows always slipping first st of every row. Change to US #8 needle and waste cotton. Knit 1 row. Bind off. Using US #8 needle and waste cotton pick up 12 sts on other end. Knit 1 row. Bind off. Felt the strap (p.19). Pick up and knit (p.22) 12 sts on the felted strap using Lamb's Pride Worsted and US #8 needles. Use 3-needle bind off (p.20) to attach strap to bag. Repeat on other end of strap.

SELF-MADE BUTTON (p.23)

Crochet button using 1 strand of Lamb's Pride. Thread remaining stash yarn with a tapestry needle and work a few sts around the ring with a blanket stitch. Center button on bag and attach by weaving yarn through the felted bag several times.

BEADED TASSEL

Using small beading needle, thread a 12" (30.5cm) long sewing thread. Tie ends together to form a loop. Pick up large beads right side facing and pull halfway through thread length and lay on table. Split yarn ends carefully to unravel a thinner ply to pass through the bead. Insert split yarn end through loop below beads. Using beading needle pull thread through pulling yarn end

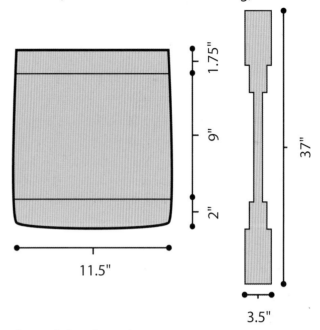

(Measurements before felting)

11.5"

1.75"

9"

2"

37"

3.5"

through beads at the same time. Pass beads up the yarn to allow a longer tail to tie several small overhand knots at the end to hold beads securely. Repeat threading up 4 or more yarn ends. Wrap yarn ends around button to desired length and tie them together to form a tassel. Pull ends through the back of the button to secure.

LOOP CLOSURE

Crochet loop using 1 strand of Lamb's Pride Worsted (p.23).

TECHNIQUES

Working with Stitch Markers (p.13)

Slipped Stitches (p.18)

Felting Wool (p.19)

Bridging Felted with Knitting (p.19)

3-Needle Bind Off (p.20)

Picking Up Stitches (p.22)

Self-Made Buttons (p.23)

Fur Loop Bag

An ultra chic, ultra sassy fur loop bag is the ideal accessory to make any outfit stand out in a crowd. The knitted fur texture gives the purse a rich looking body. Worked in simple Garter stitch, knitted loops and single crochet, this urban chic bag is the perfect companion for any party.

YARN

2 balls Berroco Suede *120yds (111m) 50g (100% nylon) Color: #3715*

1 ball Trendsetter Voila Print *208yds (192m) 50g (100% nylon) Color: #67*

1 ball Trendsetter Willow *70yds (65m) 50g (100% polyester) Color: #18*

NEEDLES

US #7 (4.5mm) 16" (40.5cm) circular needle, one spare needle US #5 (3.75 mm) and US #7 (4.5mm) short single pointed needle.

Crochet hook size F.

GAUGE

In Garter Stitch pattern 20 sts and 40 rows = 4" (10cm).

FINISHED MEASUREMENTS

12" (30.5cm) wide x 9" (23cm) tall.

HANDLES (make two)

With Suede, single crochet around the ring to completely cover. (approx 175sc.) Slip st (p.18) to close round. *Chain 1, turn, 36 sc.*

Repeat from * to *. With US #7 needles pick up and knit 36 sts.

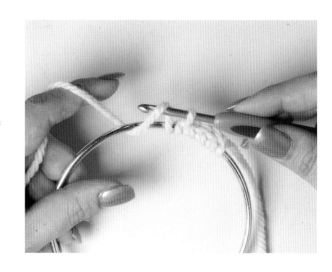

Knit one row. Continuing in Garter st inc 1 st at the beg of every row 14 times = 50 sts. Place on holder.

BODY

With US #7 needles and Suede, cast on 100 sts. Join in the round, place marker (p.13), and P1 round.

K1 round.

P1 round.

K1 round.

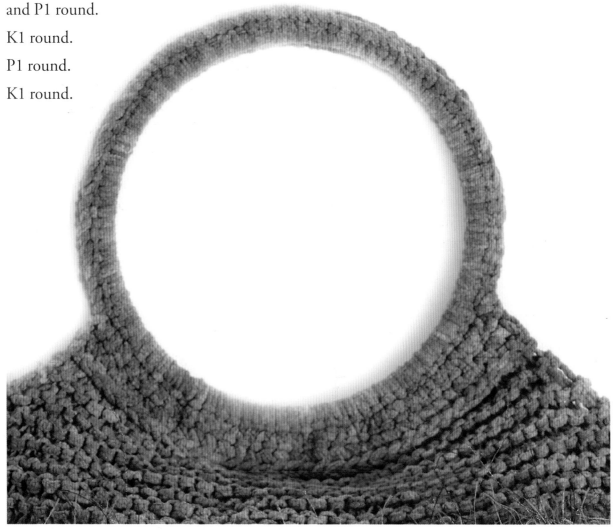

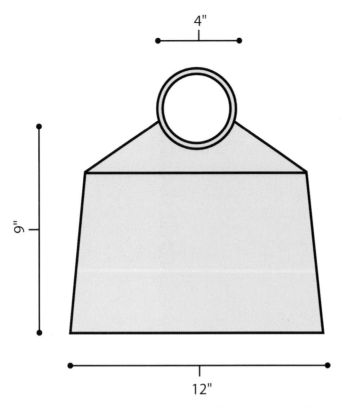

4"

9"

12"

LOOP PATTERN

Round 1: Change to 1 strand of Voila Print and Willow held tog and P1 round.

Round 2: Make loops: *K but don't drop st off left needle, yfwd, wrap around left thumb, ybk, K tbl of same st, pass first K st over second K st, P1. * Rep around. Repeat last 2 rounds until piece measures 8" (20cm) ending with row 1 followed by 1 round of P in Suede.

JOIN HANDLES

Transfer sts from holder back onto needle, wrong side facing, bind off using the 3-needle bind off (p.20) with Suede yarn. Repeat for second handle.

FINISHING

Thread a large tapestry needle with one strand of Suede, and stitch bottom together, right side facing.

TECHNIQUES

Working With Stitch Markers (p.13)

Slipped Stitches (p.18)

3-Needle Bind Off (p.20)

Yarn Resources

Manufacturers
*Wholesale only. Contact
companies for local retailers.*

Berroco, Inc.
P.O. Box 367
Uxbridge, MA 01569
tel: 508-278-2527

Blue Heron Yarns
29532 Canvasback Drive #6
Easton, MD 21601
tel: 410-819-0401

Brown Sheep Company, Inc.
100662 County Road 16
Mitchell, NE 69357
tel: 308-635-2198

Colinette, Unique Kolours
28 N. Bacton Hill Road
Malvern, PA 19355
tel: 610-644-4885

Crystal Palace Yarns
160 23rd Street
Richmond, CA 94804
tel: 510-237-9988

Gedifra and Maggi Knits, K. F. I.
PO Box 336
Amityville, NY 11701
tel: 516-546-3600

Ironstone Yarns
P.O. Box 8
Las Vegas, NM 87701
tel: 505-425-6892

Manos Del Uruguay, Design
Source
P.O. Box 770
Medford, MA 02155
tel: 781-438-9631

Mountain Colors
P.O. Box 156
Corvallis, MT 59828
tel: 406-961-1900

Muench Yarns
1323 Scott Street
Petaluma, CA 94954
tel: 707-763-9377

Naturally and Stylecraft
S. R. Kertzer Limited
50 Trowers Road
Woodbridge, Ontario L4L 7K6,
Canada
tel: 800-263-2354

Needful, King, and Lana Gatto
Needful Yarns
60 Industrial Pkwy, PMB #233
Cheektowaga, NY 14227
tel: 416-398-3700

Plassard Yarns / Brookman
Imports
105 Dixon Drive
Chestertown, MD 21620
tel: 866-341-9425

Plymouth, Lincatex and Adriafil
Plymouth Yarn
P.O. Box 28
Bristol, PA 19007
tel: 215-788-0459

Rowan
Westminster Fibers
4 Townsend W, Unit 8
Nashua, NH 03063
tel: 603-886-5041

S. Charles
70–30 80th Street / Building 36
Ridgewood, NY 11385
tel: 800-338-YARN

Trendsetter Yarn
16745 Saticoy Street / Ste 101
Van Nuys, CA 91406
tel: 818-780-5497

All accessories and yarns
available at:
Stitch Inn
5788 Route 202
Lahaska, PA 18931
tel: 215-794-4120
or online at www.stitchinn.us

ABOUT THE AUTHOR

As a yarn shop owner and teacher, I spend every day exploring knitting ideas with my customers, students, business partner, and staff.

Having a great variety of yarns to work with, it is easy to pull coordinating yarns and wonder "What should I make with these gorgeous yarns?" For me the curiosity never ends. My work is an ongoing experiment of yarns, fibers, stitches, and tools. I am grateful for being introduced to the world of stitches at the age of four by my grandparents in rural Finland.

As a child, I watched my grandmother create beautiful stitches, and I was always welcome to play with her huge scrap stashes. Growing up, my mother Daisy shared stories with me from her days of designing knitwear for her boutique and special clients. Her education in tailoring and my aspirations to work in the fashion world resulted in many home made fashion garments. I took Mom's advice and focused on business courses in college, but after seven years of working for others, I was ready to open my first needlework and yarn store. As classes filled up quickly and customers continued to come back, I knew I had found my niche.

Today, I am so proud to pass the tradition on to my 14-year-old daughter Madelaine who knits and designs wonderful fashions of her own. In October 2001, I opened my second store, Stitch Inn, in Lahaska, which sits in picturesque Bucks County, Pennsylvania. Today I manage the store with my business partner Debbie Wenclawiak, which affords me the time to write patterns and help fill our customer's knitting needs. I hope you enjoy this collection and choose to knit up some of these playful designs.

–Maria Williams

INDEX